JNANESHWAR

AMRITANUBHAV

The Nectar of Self-Awareness

A Poet's Rendering

Also by George Franklin

Prose:
Portraits from Life: A Poet's Mentors, Nicasio Press, 2022
Voicing Orpheus: On Poets and Poetry, Nicasio Press, 2022
Some Segments of a River: On Poetry, Mysticism, and the Imagination, Nicasio Press, 2020

Poetry:
Lamentations, Ristretto Books, 2024
Contour With Shadow, Frolic Press, 2016
The Fall of Miss Alaska, Six Gallery Press, 2007

Anthologies:
First Flowering: The Best of the Harvard Advocate, 1977
Roof: An Anthology of Poetry from the Naropa Institute, 1976

TRANSLATION

By George Franklin

We try to arrive at something like the truth,
And something like is the closest we ever come
When by the truth is meant a subtlest splendor
We catch brief glimpses of, as in the still
Interstices that shimmer between two thoughts,
Transforming a face into a countenance
That shines on us as, heedless, we observe it;
Then sight becomes like listening, as to the chords
Of a symphony we have come to know by heart
Whose auras ramify beyond all meaning,
Inexhaustible, untranslatable, and yet real,
And vibrate, too, in the silence between sounds,
Charged intervals in which, prolonged, suspended,
We lose and find ourselves, rapt out of time
Or deeply into it, forgetting the broken traces
That worry the surface of our waking dreams -
So I have lost and found myself, friend, in you,
Though something like is the closest I have come
When I have tried to know your subtlest truth,
A quiet splendor bright as the rising sun.

JNANESHWAR

AMRITANUBHAV

The Nectar of Self-Awareness

A Poet's Rendering

George Franklin

Cover Design:	Charles Rozier
Devanagari image:	Ms. Sarah Welch
	Own work, CC BY-SA 4.0
Cover Image:	Public Domain
Published by:	Nicasio Press
	Sebastopol, California
	www.nicasiopress.com

ISBN: 979-8-9897756-5-1
Printed in the USA

CONTENTS

PREFACE

This work in your hands is a labor of love on every level.

Amritanubhav, or *The Nectar of Self-Awareness,* was born of, and is saturated with, not only the transcendent wisdom of its author, the great thirteenth-century Indian poet-saint Jnaneshwar, but also with his intense devotion to the ever-present sacred (symbolized by Shiva and Shakti) and to his own guru and brother, Nivrittinath. Further, as George Franklin observes in his playful essay "Homage to Jnaneshwar," included in this book, *The Nectar of Self-Awareness* was also an expression of its author's compassionate love for his non-Sanskrit-speaking countrymen, for whose sake he broke with tradition by setting the text in their own vernacular language, Marathi.

The rendering of *Amritanubhav* into poetic English was also a labor of love for George Franklin, my brother. George's longstanding devotion to its author is beautifully described in his "Homage to Jnaneshwar." His profound fascination with and reverence for the text itself, as well as its author, stayed with him until his last breath. George's rendering of the text into English was also both a loving thanks-offering to his own guru, Swami Muktananda, and an act of generosity towards his English-speaking readers, for whom he rendered this exquisite text into our vernacular. George labored long and hard to capture Jnaneshwar's ecstatically poetic voice, by means of similarly poetic language in English, to evoke for us the spirit and essence of Jnaneshwar's masterpiece.

In addition, this book was a labor of love on the part of its editor and publisher, Laura Duggan, without whom it would never have seen the light of day. It is Laura whose early belief in George's rendering and desire to ensure its publication was described by George in his "Homage to Jnaneshwar" essay, and whom George referred to in that piece as "my benefactor." At various stages, Laura's ongoing support gave George the encouragement he needed to continue his efforts. George regarded her with enormous affection and respect and was deeply grateful for her friendship as well as for all she did to bring a number of his other works out into the world. Laura is not only a skilled editor but someone with a deep knowledge of the tradition George writes about, which gave her the great discernment as an editor that George prized.

After George's death, his Jnaneshwar manuscripts were initially believed to have been lost. After much searching by George's sisters and friends, his younger sister, Sheila Lieber, found a hodgepodge of sheaves of pages in a closet in George's childhood home. I examined these pages to see if they might be George's lost text, which very happily they did appear to be. Then with great care and love, Laura tirelessly cross-referenced these to piece together George's rendering of the text. Whenever Laura was unsure of something, she checked with a gifted Marathi scholar and Jnaneshwar expert, Anand Mundra, who generously offered his time and counsel as well. George's dear friend Jonathan Shimkin, one of the people whose views George most respected about both the spiritual teachings of the Shaivite tradition and also about poetics in general, read the manuscript and offered his helpful comments, too. George's brilliant elder sister and dedicated literary executor, Helena Rozier, gave her final review. Finally, Helena's husband, George's brother-in-law Charles Rozier, created a splendid cover for the book, which we all feel George would have loved.

We give great thanks to George for this sublime rendering of Jnaneshwar's inspiring and profound sacred text, and to all those mentioned above who contributed to the publication of this book in the form you see it here.

Cindy Franklin

EDITOR'S NOTE

Several years ago, while working with George on his book *Some Segments of a River,* we reminisced by email about how we first met when I had unsuccessfully attempted to have his rendering of *Amritanubhav* published. He shared the full story with me, included here as the "Homage to Jnaneshwar," in which he details the final fate of the manuscript. Spoiler alert...it was completely lost forever.

Fast forward to several months after George's passing, when, as Cindy explained in her preface, an early version of the manuscript was located among his papers. Cindy and his sisters scanned and collated the pages and sent them to me. I was thrilled, knowing how much this text had meant to George and to many of us walking a non-dual spiritual path.

I had already received emails from George indicating that he had continuously revised the translation, so it was ultimately impossible to decide which version the manuscript represented, except to know it was a work in progress. In consultation with George's family, we are printing this version as it was found, with the following changes:

- Verse numbers were added, and in some cases, verses were re-ordered to match the Marathi.
- Capitalization was standardized, using lowercase for "guru" and "seer," and uppercase for "Self," "Consciousness," and "Reality." Italics were added for most foreign words.
- Punctuation was added as needed, including em-dashes when appropriate.

We left the gendered terminology, using he/him, while recognizing that ultimately George might have done away with it. He had begun a revision that replaced "Self" with "Ultimate Reality," changing the gender to "it." However, that process was not completed, and we did not feel at liberty to proceed with it without a manuscript to work from.

Finally, a set of endnotes to form a glossary was added to assist readers who are not familiar with the tradition from which the text springs. These were not part of George's manuscript, and we hope they are a meaningful addition.

Another outstanding thing to note is that George chose to render this as poetic prose rather than in verse form. As his friend and fellow writer Jonathan Shimkin shared with us,

> I think the prose lineation was a decision George made to value precision in the rendering of the poem's analogies and the momentum of its argument over preservation of the Marathi verse form. The text unfolds with a poetic logic of its own, which George has captured so well. And with his characteristic elegance of diction and syntax, it reads like poetry in any case.

Because the content of *Amritanubhav* deals with the indescribable Mystery, we value George's intuitive and experiential approach to rendering the text. Rather than reading for precise literal accuracy, we encourage readers to hold it as George said he did, "…catching only traces, glimmerings of the meaning of the text, of the state out of which it emerged and to which it referred."

It is a great honor to publish this poetic rendering and fulfill the vision of what George created from an act of pure devotion.

Laura Duggan

Homage to Jnaneshwar

George's words about this homage, from an email, 2020:

Enclosed is a brief chapter, "Homage to Jnaneshwar," that I wrote before my book, *Some Segments*. I like this chapter. It gives a very brief account of Jnaneshwar's life and of *Nectar*, then recounts a number of extraordinary twists and turns in my failed attempts to publish my translation and commentary on *Nectar*. This story seems to be too strange to be true, but in fact is true. The tone of the piece is playful and fun, hopefully in the same way *Nectar* is playful and fun. It occurred to me that you might enjoy reading something of mine that is lighthearted!

HOMAGE TO JNANESHWAR

Surely *Jnaneshwar* is not a name with which you, my reader, are familiar. Nor, until one fateful day, was it familiar to me. *Ah, Jnaneshwar, what a strange, a surpassingly strange, history we have had together!*

As it happened, we were formally introduced by my guru. One morning, he beckoned to me to approach his perch in the courtyard. The first and last time I received such a summons. "There is a book that you should read," he said. His translator handed me a piece of paper. On it were written the words, *The Amritanubhav of Jnaneshwar*. "You can find it," she said, "in the library."

Before long, I had learned much about you. You were the second of four siblings. Your older brother, Nivrittinath, was your guru. You were born a Brahmin. Your father left your mother to take up life as an ascetic. Sent back to his householder duties by his guru when he found out, he was persecuted ruthlessly by the Brahmin establishment, which demanded he end his life as repentance, which he did. Not long afterward, your mother, heartbroken, also died. However, insisting that you and your siblings remained disgraced by your father's sins, the establishment continued their persecution of you and your siblings, stripping you of your status as a Brahmin. At a young age, you appeared before a Brahminical court of appeals. While there, you had a buffalo recite long, sometimes particularly obscure, passages from the Vedas. The judges, stunned and abashed, marveling at your superior powers, agreed to reinstate you as a Brahmin. You refused their offer. At the age of nineteen, you composed a voluminous verse commentary on the *Bhagavad Gita* called *Jnaneshwari*. Although you were fluent in Sanskrit, you—like Dante, who was your exact contemporary, and who wrote the *Divine Comedy* in Italian rather than Latin—chose to write *Jnaneshwari* in the vernacular, in Marathi. Indeed, *Jnaneshwari* is considered not only the foundational text of

Marathi literature but its chief glory. Several years later, your guru commanded you to write, not a commentary, but an original work describing your own spiritual experiences, your state of enlightenment. You complied. The result was *Amritanubhav*, often translated as *The Nectar of Self-Awareness*, the text that my guru instructed me to read.

Soon your life took yet another turn. Although already recognized as a great and learned saint, possessed of an unparalleled intellect, you also extolled the Bhakti tradition, which stressed divine love and devotion as a complete path to the highest truth. You participated in the yearly ecstatic pilgrimages to the temple of Lord Vitthal, a form of the god Krishna, in Pandharpur. You and your fellow pilgrims, mostly ordinary householders, chanted the name of the god all day and all night until you reached the temple, where you chanted still more, before finally partaking of a celebratory feast. It was during this time in your life that you wrote your *abhangas*, ecstatic hymns in praise of Lord Vitthal, that continue to be sung to this day. At the age of twenty-two, you decided that your work in this world was complete, and that it was time to take *samadhi*.[1] You chose the auspicious time and place—the Shiva temple in your native town of Alandi at sunset. You summoned your family, friends and devotees, who gathered around you one last time. You entered a cave underground, went into a state of deep meditation, and thus passed from this world...

Jnaneshwar, my beloved Jnaneshwar, after immediately heading to the library, I asked for and received a copy of *Amritanubhav*. Almost from the first page, I was captivated and enthralled. This was the vision of spirituality, these were the words, that I had hungered for. As I read, I had a powerful feeling of recognition, almost of déjà vu, as though I were encountering a dear friend whom I had not seen for years. My guru certainly must have foreseen the effect that this small book, just over a hundred pages, would have on me.

* * *

Amritanubhav is, among other things, a brilliant, supremely witty, playfully dismissive critique of "folk-Vedanta," the Vedanta philosophy as it was understood among Brahmins in Jnaneshwar's day. As I continued to read *Amritanubhav*, I noticed that I was experiencing a familiar *rasa*, or emotional flavor, relishing something that sounded like the world view of the non-dual Shaivism of Kashmir. Had Jnaneshwar, in his wanderings throughout northern India, perhaps even venturing as far as Kashmir itself, encountered this system? Many scholars think it likely. Indeed, in *Amritanubhav*, Jnaneshwar cites as scriptural authorities, aside from one reference to the *Bhagavad Gita*, only the *Shiva Sutras* and the *Spanda Karikas*, the foundational texts of Kashmir Shaivism.

Ah, but it was not primarily the matter of the text, but its manner that so profoundly fascinated me. *Amritanubhav* consists of a long series of verse aphorisms, all identical in form. The poem is not poeticized philosophy in the manner of Lucretius' *De Rerum Natura*, perhaps its closest Western analogue. No, *Amritanubhav* works fully *as a poem*. The poem is written in the Ovi meter, devised by Jnaneshwar himself, a tight, four-lined rhyming stanza, with the final line half the length of the others. Each stanza is like a small, impossibly compact, tightly wrapped virtual bomb which, when detonated, is harmless to everything except conventional cant. Its language is gloriously, extravagantly figurative.

At the same time, and equally, it is a cogent philosophical critique. The verses, though carefully reasoned and ordered, feel, as a result of their dazzling wit, almost casual, offhand. Yet there is something magisterial, even supremely, self-confidently aristocratic in their tone. They partake of a quality akin to the Italian *sprezzatura*, a word much used during the Renaissance, which connotes the accomplishment of a difficult task that is pulled off with apparent ease. All of these traits, in addition to the playfulness of the verses, suggest, in Wallace Stevens' phrase, "the figure of the youth as virile poet." *Amritanubhav*, for all its profundity, has a youthful freshness, at times even a cheekiness about it, suggesting that it is the performance of charmingly confident young man. According to legend, Jnaneshwar delivered the poem extemporaneously before a large crowd in the public square of Alandi as a scribe busily wrote it down. This would seem to be an impossible feat. But who knows? In any case, the legend suggests the high regard in which Jnaneshwar was held.

As to the verses themselves... Each felt to me like a brilliantly tied figurative knot that dissolved as soon as I touched it, leaving merely the barest trace of knowledge and meaning behind. Moving on to the next verse, the next knot, I touched it in turn, and the same phenomenon occurred. Over and over again, in reading *Amritanubhav*, I had the brief feeling of having grasped something—some knowledge or paraphrasable meaning—followed by the feeling that I had not in fact quite grasped it. It was as though in the process of knitting something, I discovered that I could not help simultaneously unknitting it. I felt, too, to borrow a shopworn trope, as though I were wrestling with an angel, not a particularly brawny one, but a preternaturally elusive one; one who, moreover, left behind no mark, no reassuring evidence, of our encounter.

I sensed that this serial process of grasping and not quite grasping knowledge or meaning, and the disorientation it produced, was quite deliberately provoked by the text. Indeed, Jnaneshwar has great fun with debunking, in various ways, the word "knowledge" itself, especially the kind of knowledge claimed by "folk" Vedantins to produce enlightenment. The state of liberation or enlightenment exists *sui generis*; it does not require some extraneous knowledge, *thank you very much*. Nor, in fact, is "ignorance"—in Vedanta a key term used by some in a way akin to original sin in Christianity—spared similar mockery by Jnaneshwar. In an increasingly intensifying crescendo, he finally suggests that we are always already enlightened, that it is our natural state, and that we merely need to wake up to this fact.

How? Jnaneshwar mentions only one means—Consciousness' power of revelation, of grace, as bestowed, whether channeled through a guru or spontaneously, upon the disciple.

Apart from this, remarkably, the text refers to no spiritual practices whatsoever. It is not a practical guide to enlightenment but a gleeful *tour de force* that constantly cites the futility of words, mere words, to suggest this state. Nor does it respect the conventions of classical Indian philosophical texts, the solemn invocation and reiteration of the *pramanas*, the so-called valid means of proof or arguments leading to knowledge, to which all such texts must pay obeisance. Least of all does it make any reference to authority, to texts that are granted the special status of unimpeachable revelation. *Amritanubhav* is generically indeterminate, obeying no rules but its own. Instead, its force field seems to bend the very spaces in which such rules might seek refuge.

For me, *Amritanubhav* became something like an extended koan. I kept struggling, over and over again, to grasp its essence, until a kind of vexed but exhilarating exhaustion ensued. I felt I was catching only traces, glimmerings of the meaning of the text, of the state out of which it emerged and to which it referred. It occurred to me that when I let these traces dissolve, when I allowed myself a kind of radical unknowing, that I might awaken, in a flash of insight, into a deeper experience of its meaning. I never experienced such an awakening, but I did experience, from reading this remarkable poem, intimations of it.

So much for my reading, and my serial rereading, of *Amritanubhav*.

* * *

Ah, but you and I, my beloved Jnaneshwar, have had, as I have noted, a long, sometimes quite baffling (baffling to me, that is) history together.

It is now time to turn to that history, a history so strange that it could not have been invented—that is, indeed God's honest truth, down to the smallest detail, to the last jot and tittle.

The first episode I have just recounted. It is that of our having been introduced to each other by my guru, and of my subsequently encountering, *O my beloved Jnaneshwar,* your always astonishing poem.

The second episode began innocently enough. There was, at the time of which I am speaking, only one, notably stiff, scholarly translation of *Amritanubhav* into English. I decided to produce a more felicitously poetic version of the poem based on this translation. Working on this project in my spare time was highly pleasurable. When I finished it, I simply presented it to my guru as a gift. I had no further plans for it. So the poem existed, as though in the ether, in a latent state—never, I imagined, to become a patent one.

However, about ten years later, the ashram started a charitable foundation, one of whose goals was to publish new scholarly translations of heretofore untranslated, yet important, spiritual texts. *All well and good.* Then somehow the woman who was in charge of this foundation came upon a copy of my modest rendition. Or could it be that I showed it to her? With respect to this question, I suffer what is perhaps a case of selective amnesia. In any event, she read it and was quite taken by it.

Then a remarkable coincidence occurred. It was discovered that a young German man, who had been working incognito in the ashram kitchen for a year, possessed a PhD from the University of Heidelberg in East Asian Studies.[2] What had been his area of specialization? *Why, medieval Marathi, of course.* He was one of only about five Western scholars thoroughly conversant with this field. When the aforementioned head of the foundation to whom, for brevity's sake, I shall subsequently refer to as my benefactor, got wind of this, she suggested that the two of us go over my rendition. My new German friend had only one month remaining at the ashram, so we decided to concentrate on some of the thorniest verses of the text. *Again, all well and good.*

Toward the end of our month together, my benefactor decided that the foundation should publish my newly emended rendition. I began to experience a little anticipation, a little excitement about this prospect. *All very well, all very well and good.*

Soon after having made this decision, my benefactor flew to California to meet with the foundation's board of trustees, most of whom were distinguished scholars. Well, they were less than warm about my benefactor's idea of publishing my rendition. It was not, they felt, a sufficiently scholarly work, was not even translated by a scholar, and so was not in accordance with the foundation's mandate. Their position was, I suppose, understandable. My benefactor insisted that surely the foundation should occasionally publish interesting works by non-scholars. Quite a row, quite a dust-up ensued, whereupon, to my considerable disappointment, my rendition fell back to its accustomed state of etheric latency.

Many years later, I undertook a kind of fool's errand. I decided to write, largely for my own edification, a commentary on *Amritanubhav*. I soon realized I would have to research and fully understand the various philosophical systems that Jnaneshwar critiques in his poem. This required what turned out to be over a year of intense study. I then began to work on my commentary, an experience that turned out to be anything but pleasurable, and which was at times exquisitely painful.

The text, with the cunning elusiveness I have described above, staunchly resisted being pinned down in any way. And yet I kept at it, gripped by something like OCD, parsing subtleties into still more subtle subtleties, not infrequently losing the thread of what I was trying to convey, until finally I began to feel that my mental balance was in some jeopardy.

No, I did not suffer a psychotic break. But I did experience a constant, unsettling, feeling of disorientation. And yet I still persevered, month after month, until, after a year, I completed this self-imposed task. How relieved I felt to be finally done with it! Somehow my little commentary had grown to consist of a hundred ungainly pages, the length of *Amritanubhav* itself. I certainly was not foolish enough to imagine that any sane publisher would go anywhere near my non-scholarly rendition of an arcane medieval Indian text with its gargantuan commentary. I thought that at some point I would simply post it on the web, the divine world-wide web.

Then a quite literally miraculous event occurred. A friend of mine suggested that I send my manuscript to a somewhat eccentric publisher in Pittsburgh who was a family friend of his. As a lark, I did indeed send it his way. On the night of the morning after this mysterious, as yet unopened, package had arrived, the publisher had a dream, a quite extraordinary dream. A beautiful dark-skinned young man with long, jet-black hair appeared, emanating an extraordinary radiance, embraced him and placed a garland of fragrant flowers over his head. Jnaneshwar was indeed reported to have been an exceptionally beautiful young man. But Jnaneshwar was not yet done with our publisher who, I should interject, was an observant Jew, and who, in accordance with prescribed practice, had placed a *mezuzah*, a decorative box containing a passage of the Torah, over the lintel of every doorway in his house. Jnaneshwar proceeded to move from room to room, garlanding, with great love and care, each and every mezuzah. The publisher was delighted, stunned, and perplexed by this dream. The following morning, he went downstairs and opened the package that had arrived the day before. He was, needless to say, quite overwhelmed when he discovered its contents and felt as though he had some kind of divine mandate to publish my text. Who knows what further blessings might accrue to him?

When I learned of the publisher's highly improbable decision, of how it had come about, and of the proposed date of the text's publication, I was thrilled. As the date grew ever closer, I felt a joyful sense of anticipation, almost like an expectant mother's. Finally, my rendition, undertaken so many years before, would see the light of day. So would my commentary.

Then, about a month before my due date, I received a call from my friend. He informed me that the publisher, due to unforeseen financial pressures, had decided to dissolve, to liquidate, his small press. My much-labored-over manuscript, once again, would have to revert to its state of etheric latency.

* * *

Ah, but as it turned out, one last chapter of this really absurd shaggy-dog story had not yet been written. While working on the aforementioned commentary, I had retreated, inauspiciously as it turned out, from my apartment in Brooklyn to my family's home, and indeed to my boyhood bedroom, in Long Island, recently abandoned after my mother's death—the better, or so I thought, to concentrate on the task at hand. After having fine-tuned my translation and finished my commentary, I decided to relinquish my apartment in Brooklyn and continue to live, for the most part, on my family homestead on Long Island.

The house there was hard by the usually placid waters of Long Island Sound. At some point, news of an impending hurricane that would make landfall near Long Island began to dominate local news coverage. Only two hurricanes had hit the area in the last several decades. They had done only minimal damage to my boyhood home.

Just before the hurricane hit, I placed the difficult-to-come-by books I had been studying, as well as my commentary, safely atop the desk in my bedroom, then retreated to higher ground, to the nearby house of my sister and her husband.

The ensuing storm, Hurricane Sandy, was far worse than had been anticipated. When it had passed, I assessed the damage. The ground floor of the house had been submerged, astonishingly, in three feet of water. My books, the hard copies of my translation and commentary, and the computer in which they had been stored, had not been spared by the incoming flood, which had assumed, for me at least, Biblical proportions. All, all, including my computer, had been destroyed. All traces of my years of hard labor had been expunged, as if by heavenly decree. As it turned out, neither my would-be, now-bankrupt publisher nor the ashram's archives had kept copies of my work. I was also rendered homeless for six months, but that is another story...

* * *

What, O what absurd hijinks, O my beloved Jnaneshwar, had you been up to all these years? First arranging for me to be introduced, in the most seductive possible way, to you and your extraordinary poem. Then manifesting, as out of thin air, a scholar of medieval Marathi at what seemed precisely the opportune moment. Then visiting the dreams of the obscure editor of a minor publishing house and extravagantly blessing him. Then drowning and expunging my text and commentary in an unprecedented deluge—years of work obliterated in one fell swoop.

It was not lost on me, my beloved, that you had never visited *my* dreams. In any case, a clear pattern became evident to me— you dangled before me, then withdrew, and yet again dangled before me, then withdrew again, the prospect of my work being published. Something like the simultaneous knitting and unknitting that I referred to earlier had been taking place.

Certainly, my beloved, it would not have done you any harm had my little work been published. And it might, I imagined, have done me some good.

For a time, of course, I was disconsolate.

Then it all became clear. All these years you had been, as it were, playing with me, teasing me, and seeing if I could take this game, as all other games, a little less seriously. One night I woke up proclaiming, with a delirious delight, *God is playing with me! God is playing with me!* Not *God has been destroying my ego,* or any other such grim and portentous nonsense. Who would wake up shouting that? As soon as this none-too-brilliant but altogether pleasant insight struck me, I felt tremendous relief. At last, I could return to loving you with no ulterior motive. At last, I could read your gorgeous poem without the impossible burden of feeling the need to comprehend it. Our relationship could once again be as innocent and loving as on the day we first met...

* * *

Since that time, I have continued to feel great reverence for you, not just for your extraordinary books, but for your extraordinary life. I think of you as that beautiful young man, not simply a saint but a literary genius, who composed two classic texts in his teens and early twenties, then embraced the Bhakti movement, fully immersing himself in the simple path of love, and who finally, at the age of twenty-two, decided to pass from this world surrounded by his loving friends and disciples. A figure of great sublimity and of beauty. And I continue to hope that one day—why not?—you will deign to show up in one of *my* dreams...

O, and Jnaneshwar, my beloved Jnaneshwar, not even you can unpublish these words I have written in praise of you.

Amritanubhav

By Jnaneshwar

Invocation

I take shelter in the deity known as the glorious Nivrittinath,
who is pure bliss itself,
who is unborn, imperishable, and indescribable.

I pay homage to that divine principle,
known in the world as the guru,
whose command is ever-victorious,
and who overflows with compassion.

Shiva and Shakti[3] are identical but frequently appear as two;
it is difficult to know
which aspect of each is united with which aspect of the other.

I bow to the limitless primordial parents of the universe,
who reveal their essential unity to each other,
so that I may experience that same unity.

I salute that perfect *Shambu*[4] who causes the
creation, maintenance, and destruction of the world,
who manifests as its beginning, middle, and end,
and in whom all three are dissolved.

I. SHIVA AND SHAKTI

1. I pay my respects to the God and Goddess, the unlimited, timeless parents of the universe.

2. The lover himself, out of overflowing love, becomes the beloved, and the beloved becomes the lover. Abiding in the same charming spot, they are made of the same substance and share the same food.

3. Out of intense longing, each consumes the other, then emits the other for the rapture of being two.

4. Being either one or two is sufficient to neither. We cannot really say what they are!

5. How intense is their desire to enjoy each other. Through that very desire they become one, and never allow their unity to be disturbed—not even in jest!

6. They are so averse to the pangs of separation that not even their child, the universe, can disturb their union.

7. Though they behold all of nature, both animate and inanimate, within them, they do not recognize a third.

8. Seated on the same ground, wearing the same garment of light, they dwell as one in the bliss of eternal solitude.

9. Difference itself, seeking to enjoy duality, is drawn to their intimate union, and merges with them instead.

10. It is through Lord Shiva that Shakti exists as a Goddess; yet without her, he can nowhere be found. The very existence of each is due to the other.

11.   O, how sweet and mysterious is their union! The whole universe is too small to contain them, yet they dwell together happily even in the tiniest particle!

12.   Each regards their spouse as their very life's breath, and neither creates so much as a blade of grass without the help of the other.

13.   These two alone dwell together in the house of the universe. When the master sleeps, the mistress remains as if awake and performs the roles of both.

14.   Should the master awaken, however, the whole house and everything in it is consumed.

15.   Withdrawing into solitude, they abide in unity; in the unfolding of diversity, each becomes the identical half of one whole.

16.   With respect to each other, each is both subject and object; thus they revel in each other's company.

17.   In solitude, Shiva alone dwells in the nominally different forms of male and female. From these two, the entire universe springs.

18.   As two lutes produce one note; two flowers, one fragrance; two lamps, one light;

19.   As two lips utter one word and two eyes behold one vision, so Shiva and Shakti pervade the whole of creation.

20.   Thus the eternal couple, even while manifesting duality, savor a dish of the same flavor.

21.   The devoted Shakti cannot live without her Lord; without her, the Almighty One becomes powerless.

22. His appearance is due to her, and her existence is due to him. How, then, can the two be distinguished?

23. Can one separate sugar from its sweetness, camphor from its fragrance?

24. Trying to gather the rays of a lamp, we grasp its flames instead; while trying to capture her essence, we discover him.

25. The sun appears because of its radiance, while the source of that radiance is nothing but the sun. In the same way, all difference is eclipsed by the light of the one supreme beauty.

26. An object is imaged by its reflection; from the reflection one infers its object. As the one object appears to be two, so the one Reality shines as two.

27. Without her, the Lord would be as unknowable as the void; without him, she would be devoid of herself.

28. Shakti herself has been formed by Shiva; yet without her, his life's breath, he would forfeit his characteristic nature.

29. Out of himself, Shiva creates Shakti's form; yet her form causes the Lord and all his glory to manifest as the play of the world.

30. Chagrined by the invisibility of her husband, she clothes him with a resplendent garment embroidered with his names and forms.

31. Where there was scarcity in unity, she playfully creates abundance in diversity.

32.   Dissolving her body, she reveals the glory of her Lord.
        Rendering himself anonymous, he assures her renown.

33.   Out of his intense desire to see her, he becomes the seer;
        when he sees her no longer, he becomes blind.

34.   In order to embrace her, he assumes the form of the
        universe; without her, he is left naked.

35.   He is so subtle that, even though manifest, he remains
        invisible; to humor her, he assumes the form of the
        universe.

36.   When awakened by her, his hunger is stirred; she serves
        him all that is knowable, herself included.

37.   While her husband sleeps, she gives birth to the universe
        of animate and inanimate objects; when she sleeps, her
        husband himself disappears.

38.   When her husband hides, only she can find him. Indeed,
        each of them is like a mirror that reveals the other.

39.   Shiva enjoys his own bliss by embracing her. Without her,
        he enjoys nothing at all.

40.   Shakti is the radiant form of Shiva. Shiva's love is the
        inner beauty that makes her glow. Blended together, they
        relish the banquet of their love.

41.   Wind and its swiftness, gold and its luster, cannot be
        separated; in the same way, Shiva and Shakti are
        inseparably one.

42.   To Shakti, Shiva is all. They can no more be parted than
        musk and its fragrance, fire and its heat.

43.   If day and night could travel to the abode of the sun, both
        of them would vanish in its light. In the same way, the
        apparent duality of Shiva and Shakti vanishes in their
        essential unity.

44.   So great is their union, they are even averse to that state
        from which sprouts the sacred syllable *Om.*

45.   Jnanadeva says: I bow to Shiva and Shakti who, by
        consuming the sweet dish of name and form, reveal the
        light of their underlying essence.

46.   Through their embrace, both vanish into light, and
        duality is banished just as darkness is dispelled by dawn.

47.   Just as both the ocean and the Ganges vanish into the
        great flood of cosmic dissolution, so *para* and *vaikhari*[5]
        fall silent as they discover their true nature in the union of
        Shiva and Shakti.

48.   Wind dissolves into the stillness of the sky. Both the sun
        and its light disappear into the greater light of the cosmic
        flood that dissolves the universe.

49.   Similarly, in the process of trying to behold Shiva and
        Shakti, both the seer and the seen vanish into their light.
        Again and again, I pay homage to the sole inhabitants of
        the universe!

50.   They are like a stream in which the knower drowns,
        thereby losing himself as he tries to drink the waters of
        the known.

51.   Indeed, if I imagine that I remain separate from Shiva and
        Shakti in order to pay them homage, it is a meaningless
        separation, born of words whose very distinctions they
        annihilate.

52.   And yet my salutation is like a golden ornament which, though not different from gold, honors its beauty.

53.   When the word "tongue" is uttered by the tongue, is there any difference between the word and the object denoted by it?

54.   When the ocean and the Ganges merge, their names can still be distinguished, but does it cause any difference in their intermingled waters?

55.   The sun is both the subject and object of its own illumination, but its unity is not thereby disrupted.

56.   When moonlight brightens the moon or when a lamp is revealed by its own light, is their essential nature forfeited?

57.   When the luster of a pearl plays upon it, its beauty and purity are only enhanced.

58.   Is the sacred syllable *AUM*[6] deprived of its unity because it is formed by three letters? Is the letter "N" divided into three parts because it is formed by three lines?

59.   As long as its unity is not disrupted and an added grace is attained, is there any reason why the surface of the sea should not exult in its efflorescence into radiant ripples?

60.   It is with the same delight that, not differentiating between Shiva and Shakti, I pay homage and bow before them.

61.   When a mirror is withdrawn, the image that appeared in it merges with its source. Waves vanish when the wind grows still.

62. A man comes to himself when he wakens from sleep. In the same way, I have come to myself by laying my ego at the feet of Shiva and Shakti.

63. Surrendering its separated form, salt merges with the ocean; in the same way, by surrendering my ego, I have come to my true nature as the God and his Goddess.

64. Thus I have paid homage to Shiva and Shakti by uniting with them—just as the hollow inner space of the plantain tree merges with the space outside it when its husk is stripped away.

II.   HOMAGE TO NIVRITTINATH

1.   I bow to him who is the wellspring that waters the garden of *sadhana*,[7] who is the auspicious thread of divine command, and who, though formless, is the embodiment of compassion.

2.   He mercifully hastens to rescue Pure Consciousness when, experiencing limited selfhood in an animal's body, it is trapped in the jungle of delusion.

3.   I bow to my guru Nivrittinath, who, slaying the rogue elephant in the form of *maya*,[8] offers a seeker the secret pearl of Divine Consciousness hidden in her temple.

4.   Through the guru's auspicious glance, bondage becomes liberation, and the knower recognizes his true nature.

5.   In distributing the gold of liberation, he acknowledges no difference between great and small; he grants the vision of the knower to all.

6.   His powers surpass even those of Shiva! He is the mirror in which the Self beholds his own bliss.

7.   Through his grace, the various phases of the moon of spiritual knowledge coalesce in the playful effulgence of the full moon.

8.   He is like the sea into which the Ganges flows, becoming still. All of the seeker's efforts cease as soon as he meets the guru.

9.   In his absence, the seer wears the variegated garment of appearance; as soon as he appears, all diversity vanishes.

10.   At the touch of one ray of his grace, the darkness of
       ignorance becomes the blessed daylight of self-knowledge.

11.   Through a mere sprinkling of the water of his grace, the
       Self becomes so pure that he regards even the state of
       Shiva as impure, and does not deign to be touched by it.

12.   He surrendered the greatness of his formless state to save
       his disciples, yet his true greatness never abandons him.

13.   Finding no joy in solitude, the guru, pretending to wait
       for a disciple, waits for himself to appear.

14.   Through a touch of his grace, the poison of ignorance is
       transformed into the nectar of infinite knowledge.

15.   His awareness swallows the knower himself as soon as he
       touches the knowable; even so, it suffers no impurity.

16.   With his help, the individual is exalted above even
       Brahman;[9] without it, *Brahman* himself becomes as
       insignificant as a blade of grass.

17.   Those who persevere in their efforts, regarding his will as
       supreme, attain the ripe fruits of their efforts.

18.   Unless the spring of the guru's glance enlivens the garden
       of the Vedas, no fruit will present itself to the seeker's
       hand.

19.   At his mere glance, the world of appearance recedes and
       vanishes; though his conquest is great, he refuses to call it
       his own.

20.   Humbling himself, he assumes the role of guru because of
       the unworthiness of the disciple; he is thereby entitled to
       destroy that which does not exist.

21.   He is like a raft who saves a swimmer from drowning in nonexistent water; the "individual" thus rescued remains nowhere to be found.

22.   The ordinary sky is mere space bounded by the horizon; but the great sky of the guru is limitless awareness.

23.   The brilliance of the rays of the sun, the coolness of the reflected rays of the moon—all are due to one ray of his light.

24.   The guru is like an astrologer whom Shiva, weary of his game of assuming limited forms, consults to find the auspicious time to regain his true status.

25.   He is like the moon, except that he is clothed by the glow of his own light.

26.   Though manifest, he remains unseen; though light, he does not illumine; though existent, he exists nowhere.

27.   Why, then, should I continue to infer his existence, using such words as "he" or "who?" As the ground of all *pramanas,*[10] all of the means of valid knowledge and their proofs, he is answerable to none.

28.   He remains indescribable; words become silent before his oneness that admits no intruder.

29.   Never an object of knowledge, he reveals himself as self-evident when all the *pramanas* cease to exist. Indeed, his affinity for nonexistence is wonderful!

30.   Though we may wish to catch a glimpse of him, our seeing itself pollutes his kingdom!

31.   How can I enter that kingdom by praising him or talking about him? He has renounced his name by assuming it.

32.   The Self neither approaches himself nor withdraws from himself. Nevertheless, assuming the form of the guru, he dons the transparent veil of his name.

33.   But how can he rightly be called Nivritti,[11] "renunciation?" How can he renounce anything when there is nothing to be renounced?

34.   Does the sun ever perceive darkness? Of course not! Yet it is called the enemy of darkness.

35.   Through his miraculous sport, the imagined becomes real, the inanimate becomes animate, and impossible events become possible.

36.   O venerable guru, you manifest appearances through your amazing power, then spurn them as mere chimeras. Yourself beyond all appearance, you refuse to become the object of perception.

37.   O true guru, how can I penetrate your mystery? You elude my every attempt to conceive of you!

38.   Through your power you have created and dissolved countless names and forms. And you are still not satisfied!

39.   You sacrifice the individuality of whomever you befriend; and yet, though your servant loses himself, he finds himself again due to your mastery.

40.   In truth, we cannot even call you "the Self"; you do not permit us to transform you into a name or an object.

41. There is no night for the sun; salt is dissolved in water; sleep vanishes when the sleeper awakens;

42. Camphor is consumed by fire; so name and form vanish in the guru's presence.

43. When I try to bow to him, he does not remain before me as the object of my salutations. He remains unpersuaded by any mode of difference.

44. With respect to itself, the sun does not rise. How, then, could he be exalted by one bowing before him?

45. No one can appear before him as separate from himself. Of what use is my reverence?

46. No reflection is seen in the mirror of the sky. He accepts no difference between the two of us.

47. Well, let him not be an object of worship! Why should I feel it uncanny that no trace remains of whoever comes before him?

48. When the outside of a garment is loosened, the inside is loosened as well.

49. When the guru refuses to be his object, the disciple ceases to be a subject. His individuality is effaced.

50. Sight becomes useless when there is nothing to see. We are placed in such a predicament by the guru's feet.

51. The flame of a lamp is sustained by wick and oil. It cannot be sustained by a piece of camphor.

52. The instant that camphor and flame are united, both disappear.

53.   The instant I see the guru, both of us vanish, as dreams dissolve when a sleeper awakens.

54.   Thus I have refuted the notion of duality and paid homage to the guru, my dear companion.

55.   O, how wonderful is his friendship! He has manifested the duality of master and disciple where there is no space even for unity!

56.   He is intimately related to himself without recourse to any other. He is not and does not become different from himself.

57.   Having become as great as the infinite sky, he bears the whole universe, including the night of nonexistence, within him.

58.   The nature of the ocean is fullness, but it cannot be filled. Such contradictions live happily in the house of the guru.

59.   There is no intimacy between light and darkness, yet they become one in the sun.

60.   The same "One" exists in different forms yet remains unalterably One; thus apparent contradictions contradict themselves.

61.   The words "guru" and "disciple" refer to one reality. The guru alone exists in both forms.

62.   Whether in an unworked state or in an ornament, gold is still gold. Moonlight is shed by the moon, whether full or partial.

63.   Camphor and its fragrance are nothing but camphor; sugar and its sweetness are nothing but sugar.

64. In the same way, although the guru and the disciple appear as two, it is the guru alone who masquerades as both.

65. When a person looks at himself in the mirror, he knows that his reflection is not his actual face.

66. One who wakes from sleep with no one beside him knows that he is both the awakened and the awakener.

67. Just as the awakened is the awakener, it is the one true Self who both receives knowledge and imparts it. Thus the guru-disciple relationship is upheld.

68. If the eye could behold itself without a mirror, I could describe this sport of the guru.

69. Thus the guru nourishes deep intimacy with the disciple, without admitting duality or disturbing unity.

70. Nivritti is my guru's name; Nivritti is his splendor; Nivritti is the glory of his kingdom.

71. My Nivritti is not like the word "nivritti," which is employed to oppose activity and advocate inactivity.

72. He is not like this so-called "nivritti" defined as the mere opposite of worldly activity, which is then renounced as the night, by sacrificing itself, brings about day.

73. He is the pure and supreme Lord, not a jewel that shines with a borrowed light.

74. The beauty of the sun is enhanced by its own light, and thereby it beautifies the entire world.

75.   Nivritti is the cause of his being Nivritti. He is like a flower that transforms himself into a nose to inhale his own fragrance.

76.   If eyesight were able to turn back on itself and behold the seer's face, would there be any need of mirrors?

77.   When night vanishes and day arises, does the sun strive to become itself?

78.   The guru is not like an ordinary object of knowledge. He requires no proof. No doubt can withstand him.

79.   Thus I have paid homage to the holy feet of my guru whose stillness is absolute, not the opposite of action.

80.   Having paid my respects to the guru, I have discharged the debts of all four levels of speech.[12]

III.   Discharging the Debt of Speech

1.   Speech, which awakens the Self by its clamor, cannot fully discharge its debt, for it merely awakens the Self into a kind of sleep.

2.   Though the four levels of speech—*para* and the rest—are useful for the salvation of the individual soul, when its ignorance is finally obliterated they, too, are destroyed.

3.   Just as, after death, the hands and feet are incinerated with the rest of the body, or as the subtle senses depart along with the mind, or as the sun's rays vanish with the setting sun,

4.   Or as dreams disappear when sleep ends, so the four levels of speech are annulled upon the cessation of ignorance.

5.   When iron is consumed in a furnace, it continues to exist as a medicinal cure; when fuel is consumed, it leaps upward as fire;

6.   When salt dissolves in water, it persists as taste; when sleep is dispelled, the sleeper remains in the waking state.

7.   In the same way, when the four levels of speech are destroyed, they continue to exist in the form of Pure Knowledge.

8.   The sole purpose of their sacrifice is to light the lamp of knowledge, but this knowledge itself is tiresome and vain.

9.   When sleep arrives, it shows us dreams; when it departs, we become aware of ourselves; both kinds of knowledge arise from sleep.

10.   When ignorance persists, it causes invalid perceptions; when it perishes, it grants us valid perceptions.

11.   But whether persisting or perishing, this word "ignorance" entangles us with false notions about freedom and bondage.

12.   If freedom itself is a kind of bondage, why should the word "freedom" be applied to it?

13.   A child is relieved by the death of a bogeyman. For an adult, it has never existed. Should he exult in its demise?

14.   Should we call him wise who deplores the shattering of a nonexistent vase?

15.   If bondage itself is unreal, can the freedom that arises from its destruction be real?

16.   In the *Shiva Sutras*, Lord Sadashiva has declared that knowledge itself is bondage.

17.   We do not accept this statement merely because it has been uttered by Shiva or Krishna. Regardless, it would be evident from our own experience.

18.   In the *Gita*, Shri Krishna has explained how the quality of *sattva*[13] binds one with the fetters of knowledge.

19.   If the Self, which is Pure Knowledge itself, required some further knowledge, it would be like the sun begging help from a lamp.

20.   The Self's status as Pure Knowledge would be a charade if its greatness depended upon some extrinsic knowledge. One candle requires another to enlighten it only if its own flame has guttered.

21.   Does a person forget his own existence and wander far and wide in search of himself?

22.   Does he ever exclaim that he is delighted to remember himself after the lapse of so many days?

23.   If the Self, who is Pure Knowledge itself, suddenly supposes he has attained real knowledge of himself, and proclaims "I am He," that so-called "knowledge" is nothing but bondage.

24.   Such knowledge is like one who half-drowns himself and then emerges triumphant, claiming to have liberated himself.

25.   Therefore, the four levels of speech, which are ornaments of the four bodies,[14] vanish along with ignorance when the egotism of the individual self is destroyed.

26.   When ignorance, downcast, enters the fire of Pure Knowledge, only the ashes of understanding remain.

27.   When camphor is dissolved in water, it becomes invisible but remains as the water's fragrance.

28.   When ashes are smeared on a body, its particles fall away, but a white tint is left.

29.   A stream may run dry, but its moisture persists in the nearby soil.

30.   At noon a person's shadow becomes invisible, but it still exists beneath his feet.

31.   So knowledge, which swallows everything other than itself, remains as a kind of residue even after having been swallowed itself by the ultimate reality.

32.   Not even by their self-sacrifice are the four levels of speech
       enabled to discharge their debt to the Supreme Self. I have
       discharged it by bowing my head to the sacred feet of my
       guru.

33.   When the four levels of speech—*para, pashyanti,
       madhyama,* and *vaikhari*—are destroyed, they cling to
       that knowledge which is itself a kind of ignorance.

IV. KNOWLEDGE AND IGNORANCE

1. Does knowledge reign supreme after annihilating ignorance just as wakefulness triumphs after conquering sleep?

2. Or is knowledge like a face that becomes aware of its own existence, which has never vanished, only when reflected by a mirror?

3. Such knowledge, which reveals the identity of the self and the world by separating them, is like a knife that fatally stabs itself.

4. It is like one who enters a house and sets it on fire, thus incinerating both himself and the house, or like a thief who ties himself in a bag along with his stolen goods,

5. Or like a flame that burns itself out in the process of burning camphor. So knowledge destroys itself in the process of destroying ignorance.

6. When the support of ignorance is withdrawn, knowledge spreads itself so thin that it dissolves.

7. As a wick burns to its end, its flame flares with an added brightness, but this effulgence is the harbinger of its imminent extinction.

8. At their moment of greatest ripeness, a woman's breasts begin to fall; the moment of a jasmine's blooming is that of its fading;

9. The formation of a ripple signals its erasure; lightning flashes and fades simultaneously.

10. Knowledge grows by drinking the waters of ignorance and collapses when its last dregs are consumed.

11. The cosmic deluge envelops both oceans and continents.

12. Should the disk of the sun become larger than the universe, both darkness and light would be subsumed in a greater light.

13. Should wakefulness destroy sleep only to destroy itself, both would be lost in a state of higher awareness.

14. In the same way, knowledge shines by the support of its opposite—ignorance—until both are consumed by the light of Absolute Knowledge.

15. Such Knowledge is like the full moon, except that it never wanes.

16. It can only be compared to the sun, which can neither be overwhelmed by any other luminary nor cast into darkness.

17. In the same way, Absolute Knowledge can neither be enlightened by any kind of relative knowledge nor darkened by ignorance.

18. Can knowledge know itself? Can the eyeball see itself?

19. Can the sky enter the sky, or fire burn fire? Can a person climb onto his own head?

20. Can vision survey itself, or taste taste itself, or sound hear itself?

21. Can the sun behold itself? Can fruit devour itself? Can fragrance smell itself?

22. Consciousness itself cannot be made conscious of itself.

23. If knowledge requires the aid of some other knowledge, it is really ignorance.

24. What is light is not darkness. But is the light a light to itself?

25. In the same way, he [the Self] is neither "existence" nor "nonexistence." Some might infer that he is nonexistent.

26. But if he is taken to be nothing, who knows that he is nothing?

27. Nihilism must negate existence. On what grounds, then, can it be proved?

28. If the extinguisher of light is extinguished along with the light, who knows there is no light?

29. If a sleeper were to perish during dreamless sleep, how could he tell that his sleep was sound?

30. A pot is perceived as a being a pot. When shattered, it appears as destroyed. But would anyone claim that it never existed?

31. He who perceives that nothing exists does not himself become nothing.

32. The Self has a unique existence, beyond existence or non-existence.

33. It is an object neither to itself nor to any other. Should it therefore be regarded as not existing?

34.   A person who sleeps alone in a forest is not perceived by any other, nor is he conscious of himself, but no one would claim that he does not exist.

35.   When vision turns inward, it no longer perceives outer objects, but does it cease to exist or to be aware?

36.   If a man with jet black skin were to stand in pitch darkness, neither he nor anyone else would be able to see him. Does he therefore doubt his existence?

37.   The Self's existence or nonexistence is not like that of a person.

38.   When the sky is clear of clouds, it is void of form. Though one who regards it perceives only emptiness, the sky is still the sky.

39.   When one gazes at the motionless waters of a well, the surface seems to disappear, but the water remains as it is.

40.   The Ultimate Reality abides as it is in itself, and transcends such ordinary opposites as "existence" and "nonexistence."

41.   It is like a wakefulness that bears no relationship to sleep, and therefore is not aware of itself as wakefulness, though it remains aware.

42.   Place a jar on the ground, and it can be called "the ground with a jar." Remove it, and it can be called "the ground without a jar."

43.   But in truth, it is simply the ground. In the same way, the Self, never an object and free of all qualities and their negation, simply exists as itself.

V.   EXISTENCE, CONSCIOUSNESS, AND BLISS

1.   A poison, being itself a poison, cannot poison itself; it is not three separate things. In the same way, existence, consciousness, and bliss, as separate attributes, cannot determine the Self.

2.   Luster, hardness, and yellowness together constitute gold; sweetness, stickiness, and thickness together constitute honey.

3.   Whiteness, softness, and fragrance together constitute camphor.

4.   Camphor is white; its whiteness is soft; its whiteness and softness are fragrant.

5.   Just as these three together constitute camphor, and have no separate existence as a triad, similarly existence, consciousness, and bliss are all merged in one Reality.

6.   Existence, consciousness, and bliss are different as three words, but their nominal existence is blithely annulled by the Self.

7.   Is *existence* bliss and consciousness, or is *consciousness* existence and bliss?

8.   The moon, appearing to us on earth, seems to pass through different stages of fullness. But in itself, the moon is always full.

9.   When water is falling in drops, we can count them. But can we count the drops in the puddle that forms where it falls?

10.   The Vedas call the Absolute "existence" so that it cannot be called "nonexistence," "consciousness" so that it cannot be called "unconsciousness."

11.   Similarly, they proclaim the Absolute "bliss" because there is no pain in it.

12.   "Nonexistence" and its negative counterparts are the opposites of "existence" and its positive counterparts; the latter are employed to differentiate the Self from the former.

13.   Thus the term "sat-chit-anand"[15] is applied to the Self not to denote its nature, but to differentiate it from what it is not.

14.   Can the objects that are illumined by the sun illumine the sun itself?

15.   Can the organ of speech reveal that by whose light it comprehends its objects?

16.   The Self, illuminating itself, needs no further illumination; it can never become an object of knowledge. It is itself the ground of knowledge.

17.   The Self is self-evident; the means of valid knowledge are limited by, and limited to, the objects to which they apply.

18.   As we try to know the Self, knowledge itself and the known become one and merge in the Self.

19.   The words "existence," "consciousness," and "bliss" do not truly denote the Self. They are merely the verbal residue of knowledge.

20. When these well-known words are finally united with the Knower, they vanish like rainclouds after a storm has passed;

21. Or like rivers that flow into the sea; or like a path that ends when it reaches its goal.

22. A flower fades after giving rise to fruit; the fruit is lost in the process of squeezing it for juice; the juice vanishes into the satisfaction of the drinker.

23. The priest's hand is withdrawn after it offers its oblation to the sacrificial fire; the musician's hands grow still, and the melody ends after it has delighted the listener.

24. One has finished with a mirror after having seen one's face in it; a person has no need to linger after awakening a sleeper.

25. After pointing the way to the awareness of the Self, existence, consciousness, and bliss are lost in silence.

26. No matter what one calls the Self, it is not what one calls it. A person cannot measure his height by measuring the length of his shadow

27. As soon as he realizes the absurdity of this enterprise, he becomes self-aware and gives it up.

28. Existence, of course, cannot be called nonexistence, its supposed opposite. But does that which does not exist have an opposite? Can existence have any real status as the positive contrary of a nonexistent negative?

29. Similarly, can knowledge arise by destroying the absence of knowledge?

30. Where there is only wakefulness, there is neither a "sleeping state" nor a "waking state." Similarly, there is no "knowledge" in Pure Awareness.

31. Where no unhappiness or deprivation exists, what meaning is there in the term "bliss"?

32. Therefore, in the Absolute, existence vanishes along with nonexistence, knowledge along with ignorance, and bliss along with misery.

33. Renouncing the veil of duality and all pairs of opposites, the Self remains alone in its own blessedness.

34. Yet if the Self is counted as "one," it remains apart from the one who counts. So the Self is one absolutely but not numerically.

35. Only one who remains apart from bliss can be said to enjoy it. The bliss of the Self pervades itself so fully, it cannot be experienced as "bliss."

36. At the beating of the drum, the Goddess enters the body of her worshipper; but when neither are present, does the drumbeat enjoy its own sound?

37. In the same way, the Self, being bliss itself, experiences neither bliss nor the lack of it.

38. When not in front of a mirror, a person neither faces it nor turns from it; in the same way, the pure bliss of the Self is neither bliss nor non-bliss.

39. All theories regarding his nature are as irrelevant as chatter in a dream. He conceals himself even from his own understanding.

40. He is like a sweet juice that exists, even before the planting of the sugar cane, as the inner awareness of sweetness itself.

41. Even before the strings of the vina are plucked, its sound is inherent within it; but that sound is heard by itself alone.

42. Before a bee enters it, the innermost part of a flower alone is aware of its ravishing fragrance.

43. The flavor of a dish that has not yet been cooked is savored not by others, but only by that flavor itself.

44. Can bliss, too shy to enjoy its own face, be scrutinized and enjoyed by others?

45. When the moon is in the sky at noon, her presence is known only to herself.

46. The pure awareness of the Self is like beauty that has yet to assume any form, youth prior to the existence of a body, religious merit before the performance of any oblation.

47. It is like the first stirring of desire seeking erotic pleasure in a mind that does not yet exist;

48. Or like the sound of a musical instrument, as yet uncreated, that cannot be understood by verbal description, but only by the sound itself;

49. Or like a fire that spreads before contact with any fuel.

50. Only those who are able to behold their faces without using a mirror are able to grasp the secret of the self-evident Reality.

51.   Speaking in this way is like storing and harvesting a crop before its seeds have been sown.

52.   The pure awareness of the Self transcends any conception or description, forever reveling in itself.

53.   Having said this much, I can say that only that speech is wise which has drunk deep from the draught of silence.

54.   The various modes of proof have revealed their inability to prove, and analogies their inability to illustrate, the true nature of the Absolute.

55.   All arguments have dissolved in attempting to conceive it, and all definitions, having assembled in an attempt to identify it, have been routed.

56.   All modes of discourse, having proven their futility, have surrendered their object.

57.   Thought along with its judgements has perished like courageous warriors slain in the service of their master.

58.   Understanding, humiliated by its reliance on useless knowledge, has immolated itself, abandoning experience, leaving it crippled and alone.

59.   When the crust of a piece of talc has flaked away, the talc itself disappears.

60.   If the husk of a plantain tree melts in the heat, can its vacant core stand erect?

61.   Experience arises as the relation between subject and object; when both vanish, can experience experience itself?

62.   Of what use are words when experience itself has
        vanished?

63.   How can words approach the Ultimate Reality, when
        paravak, supreme speech itself, has dissolved in it, and
        no trace of any sound can be found?

64.   Should there be any talk of awakening one already
        awakened? Does one cook a meal after having eaten
        one's fill?

65.   When the sun rises, does one require a lamp? Is there
        any sense in plowing a harvested field?

66.   There is no cause either of bondage or of liberation.
        Nothing remains to be accomplished. There is only the
        joy of expression itself.

67.   When a thing is lost, due to forgetfulness, either to
        others or to ourselves, the word can serve to recall it.

68.   The word can glorify itself only by recourse to its status
        as a reminder.

VI.   THE INEFFICACY OF THE WORD

1.   The word is renowned for enabling us to recall even that which is absent. Is it not a mirror that reflects the formless?

2.   It is no surprise when visible things are reflected in a mirror. But in the magic mirror of the word, even invisible objects are seen!

3.   The word is like a rising sun that illumines all that has emerged from the Unmanifest; it even renders the sky visible.

4.   The word is the flower of the sky. Its fruit is the universe. Is there anything that cannot be measured by the word?

5.   The word is a torchbearer who illumines the path of right and wrong actions. It serves as a judge in disputes between bondage and freedom.

6.   When it sides with ignorance, the unreal appears real, and the real appears worthless.

7.   Switching sides, it becomes the exorcist who frees the finite self to penetrate the body of Shiva.

8.   It disentangles the finite self from the body. By means of the word, the Self reenters itself.

9.   The sun, at daybreak, dispels the night, its enemy. Perhaps we cannot really compare the word to the sun.

10.   After all, the word is impartial; it equally supports both parties in pairs of opposites such as "action" and "inaction."

11.   The word sacrifices itself, thereby abetting the knowledge that leads to the Self.

12.   In fact, the word is only useful as an aid to memory. It bears no relation at all to the Absolute.

13.   Absolute Consciousness, being self-luminous and without support, needs nothing to reveal it, and renders the word useless.

14.   There is nothing apart from the Self; therefore, the Self is subject neither to remembering nor to forgetting.

15.   Can one remember or forget oneself? Can the tongue either taste or fail to taste itself?

16.   There is no sleep to one who is always awake. But for him, is there such a thing as waking? Just so, neither forgetting nor remembering pertain to the Absolute.

17.   The sun does not know the night. How, then, can it be conscious of the day? What is there to be remembered or forgotten?

18.   Thus the word, useful only for recollection, is utterly useless with respect to the Self.

19.   Another purpose is imputed to the word—but I am almost embarrassed to mention it.

20.   It is preposterous to claim that the word must destroy ignorance before the Self can become conscious of itself.

21.   If one were to assert, "the sun must destroy night before it can arise," one would become a laughingstock to intelligent people.

22.   Can one either dispel the sleep of one who is already awake or awaken him?

23.   Can one destroy the nonexistent, or cause the existent to enter the state of existence?

24.   Ignorance is as unreal as the son of a barren woman. Why, then, does the axe of discrimination insist upon hacking it?

25.   If the rainbow were as real as it seems, every archer would string it and use it as a bow.

26.   One can sooner quench one's thirst on the waters of a mirage than conquer ignorance by logical thinking.

27.   Trying to annihilate ignorance through the word is like trying to immolate a city in the sky.

28.   Darkness cannot coexist with a lighted lamp. But before it was lit, was there anything there to be destroyed?

29.   Does one light a lamp to reveal the day?

30.   Does a shadow substantially exist either where it falls or where it does not fall?

31.   Upon wakening, one recognizes that images in a dream are unreal. In the same way, ignorance is unreal even though it appears to be real.

32.   Is there anything to be gained by hoarding counterfeit coins conjured by a magician, or by stealing the clothes off a naked beggar's back?

33.   Eating a thousand imaginary sweets does not break a fast.

34. The sand upon which a mirage does not appear is dry, but does it become moist when a mirage does appear?

35. Claiming that ignorance has a real existence is like claiming that the real people, lakes, and fields copied in a picture are flooded by the painted rain that falls in it.

36. If it were possible to fill one's pen with darkness, would anyone bother with ink?

37. The sky, although colorless, appears blue to the eye. The existence of ignorance is equally illusory.

38. Ignorance, by its very name, proclaims its own nonexistence.

39. Those who call ignorance "indefinable" are really admitting that there is nothing to define.

40. When a jar is placed on the earth, it leaves a mark. In the same way, what really exists cannot be determined by thought.

41. To say that the destruction of ignorance reveals the Self is like saying the destruction of a shadow reveals the light.

42. Ignorance is not merely an appearance but one that hides itself by not appearing in any form; thereby, it proves its own absence.

43. Thus, as has been indicated in various ways, ignorance is by its very nature nonexistent. What, then, remains for the illustrious word to destroy?

44. Attempting to strike a shadow, you will strike only the ground. Try hard enough, and you will succeed only in breaking your arm.

45. Seeking to thrill at the destruction of ignorance is as absurd as seeking joy by drinking the nectarean water of a mirage,

46. Or by embracing the air, or by kissing one's own reflection.

47. One might just as well, at one's leisure, flay the skin off the sky;

48. Or milk the nipples of a billy goat with one's knees, or punch a hole in the air, dry it out, and make a wafer of it;

49. Or crush a yawn to extract its juice, mix it with indolence, and pour it down the throat of a headless corpse.

50. One might as profitably reverse the flow of a river, flip one's shadow like a pancake, or twist the strands of the wind into a rope;

51. Or proceed to thrash an imaginary ogre, or stuff one's reflection into a pillowcase, or lovingly comb the hair on one's palms;

52. Or shatter a nonexistent vase, or pluck flowers from the garden of the sky, or break off the horns of a hare;

53. Or prepare ink from chalk, or sweep out the soot inside a diamond, or marry the daughter of a childless woman;

54. Or feed the birds who nest at the center of the earth with the absent rays of the new moon, or fish the waters of a mirage for aquatic unicorns.

55. What more can I say? The very nature of ignorance is nonexistence. What remains for the word to destroy?

56. Just as darkness cannot determine the nature of darkness, so the word cannot be a valid means of knowledge by destroying what does not exist.

57. This ignorance, which is called not only "indefinable" but "beginningless," has thus never been born. Disputing about it is as pointless as lighting a lamp at noon in the middle of a courtyard.

58. He who seeks to gather a harvest before sowing seeds reaps only ridicule.

59. Whoever begs alms from a naked ascetic would do better to stay at home.

60. What is the use of watering water? The same as trying to destroy ignorance through the word.

61. A ruler is useful, but not for measuring the sky. Of what use is light if it can perceive darkness?

62. The tongue is useful for discriminating certain flavors, but can it taste the air?

63. Does a woman delight in wearing her husband's favorite dress when he is no longer alive? Can one devour the empty core of a plantain tree?

64. What object, great or small, cannot be illumined by the sun? But can the sun illumine the night?

65. What object cannot be perceived by the eyes? But can even the eyes perceive the nonexistent sleep of one who is awake?

66. If the *chakor* bird[16] were to try to seek the moon at noon, his search would prove the height of vanity.

67.   When one has only a blank page to read, to be a reader is pointless. Legs are useless for running through a void.

68.   In the same way, words are reduced to meaningless chatter when they are employed to dispel ignorance.

69.   If the new moon were to arise at noon, would it obliterate darkness? To imagine that words can destroy ignorance is equally absurd.

70.   To try to eat food that has not yet been gathered is to fast. To look through blind eyes is to see nothing.

71.   In the very attempt to determine the meaning of what does not exist, the word annihilates itself.

72.   Should I even attempt to expound the nonexistence of ignorance? Nothing remains of the word that attempts to destroy it.

73.   As thought reflects upon ignorance, it, too, becomes nonexistent, and succeeds only in destroying itself.

74.   By its very nature, ignorance, being nonexistent, prevents the word from becoming the means of its destruction.

75.   Similarly, the notion that the word can shed light on the self-luminous Self is preposterous.

76.   In what country can a person marry himself? Can the sun be eclipsed by the sun?

77.   Can the sky rush to meet itself, or the ocean flow into itself, or the palm touch itself?

78. Does a second sun cause the sun to rise, or a fruit bear another fruit, or the sense of smell enjoy its own fragrance?

79. Both animate and inanimate objects can consume water, but can water drink itself?

80. Is there a day in the year when the sun can behold itself through its own eyes?

81. When the God of destruction is angry, he burns all three worlds. But can his fire burn itself?

82. Can even the creator stand before himself without aid of a mirror?

83. It is certain that sight cannot see itself, that taste cannot taste itself, that one who is already awake cannot waken himself.

84. Can sandalwood wear itself, or color paint itself, or can a pearl adorn itself with its own luster?

85. Can gold test its own purity, or a lamp light itself, or a flavor enjoy its own sweetness?

86. Lord Shiva wears the moon on his head. But can the moon perch on its own head?

87. In the same way, Consciousness, being the ground of Pure Knowledge, cannot be embraced or comprehended by knowledge.

88. Being Knowledge itself, the Self does not need to know itself any more than the eye needs to see itself.

89.   The Self can no more know itself than the surface of a mirror can reflect itself.

90.   A knife can cut almost anything, but can it cut itself?

91.   The tongue can savor all kinds of flavors, but can it taste itself?

92.   Does the tongue cease to be an organ of taste because it cannot taste itself? Of course not; it cannot taste itself because the sense of taste is immanent within it.

93.   In the same way, the Self, which encompasses Absolute Being, Knowledge, and Bliss as immanent within it, is self-evident; the word has nothing to offer it.

94.   Being self-evident, the Self is unaffected by any of the limited means of knowledge that would prove or disprove it.

95.   It is therefore futile for the word to put on airs and to claim that through its ministry, the Self comes to know itself.

96.   A lamp lit at noon neither dispels darkness nor spreads light. The effect of the word is the same with respect to the Absolute.

97.   Ignorance, being nonexistent, cannot be destroyed; the Self, being self-evident, is not amenable to proof.

98.   Thus, being useless no matter which way it turns, the word vanishes like a stream that is lost in the waters of the cosmic flood.

99.   Right thinking reveals that the word has no relationship whatever to the Self.

100.   Those who disagree might as well say that the sky hangs
        from palm fronds or that a ghost has built their home.

101.   The idea of words depicting the Self is as nonsensical as
        the idea of painting a picture with colors not found in
        nature.

102.   Notions of knowledge and ignorance, whose status
        pitifully depends upon the word, are as substantial as a
        forest sketched with a crayon.

103.   As cloudiness vanishes when clouds disappear, so both
        ignorance and knowledge vanish when the word
        disappears in the Self.

VII. The Refutation of the Doctrine of Ignorance

1. If not for the help of knowledge, the very word "ignorance" could not exist.

2. A firefly begins to shine only when darkness falls. Similarly, the notion of beginningless ignorance is a mere chimera.

3. Ignorance is real in itself only as darkness and dreams are real in themselves; it vanishes with the dawning of knowledge.

4. Horses fashioned of clay cannot be saddled; bracelets painted on canvas cannot be worn.

5. If one tries to abduct ignorance from the abode of knowledge, one's hostage will disappear. Do the waves of a mirage ripple in the moonlight?

6. Similarly, what is called "knowledge" is dependent upon ignorance.

7. But enough of these preliminaries! Let us commence our search for ignorance. By understanding its true nature, we will recognize the falsity of knowledge.

8. If ignorance really exists within knowledge, why does it not turn knowledge into ignorance?

9. Is it not the intrinsic nature of ignorance to delude the one in whom it dwells?

10. Some interpret the scriptures as asserting that ignorance, dwelling within the Self, conceals and envelops its host.

11. To them I reply: if the seed of ignorance dwells in that state in which there is no sprouting of duality, by whom could it be known?

12. Ignorance, being nescient, cannot know itself. Can that which is unconscious prove its own existence?

13. Anyone stating that ignorance causes the knowledge of ignorance would become aware of contradicting himself and would promptly fall silent.

14. If ignorance were intelligent enough to delude the Self, who would call it ignorance?

15. Is it not shameful to impute ignorance to that in which the consciousness of its own existence is never concealed?

16. If clouds could blot out the sun, could the sun illumine them? If a person were annihilated by sleep, who could remember having slept?

17. If that in which ignorance dwells became ignorant, then ignorance itself, being unable to know itself, would promptly vanish.

18. That by which ignorance is discerned can never be ignorance itself.

19. If a person has a cataract in his eye, does it make sense to say that his vision is unimpaired?

20. If fuel does not burn upon contact with a raging fire, should flammability be ascribed to it?

21. If a house remains as bright as ever when it is filled by darkness, should we still be speaking of darkness?

22.   Should we call that sleep which does not interrupt the
        waking state? Should we call that night which does not
        banish daylight?

23.   If the Self, pervaded by ignorance, still retains the
        attributes of the Self, the very word "ignorance" is
        rendered meaningless.

24.   It is clearly illogical to claim that ignorance dwells in the Self.

25.   Ignorance is a dense and impenetrable darkness. The Self
        is the source and essence of all effulgence. How is it
        possible for the two to be identified?

26.   If memory and forgetfulness, the waking and the dream
        states, could coexist in the same person;

27.   If cold and heat, journeying together, could sojourn at the
        same destination; if a bundle of the sun's rays could be
        cinched by a rope of darkness;

28.   If day and night could arrive together at the same
        destination, or life and death cohabit in the same body—

29.   Only then could the Self in any way be associated with
        ignorance.

30.   But why should it even occur to anyone to say that the
        very ignorance that is supposedly dispelled by the Self
        abides within it?

31.   When darkness, upon sunrise, surrenders its existence as
        darkness, it becomes light.

32.   When fuel, consumed by fire, surrenders its existence as
        fuel, it becomes fire.

33. When a stream, flowing into the Ganges, surrenders its existence as a stream, it becomes the Ganges.

34. Even were ignorance to exist, as soon as it came in contact with the Self, it would become Pure Knowledge.

35. Ignorance can neither abide in its antithesis—knowledge —nor can it exist independent of it.

36. Even if one could bring a fish made of salt to life, it would perish both in water and on dry land.

37. Some say, "The Self is revealed when ignorance is abolished." Ignore such idle talk.

38. Just as a serpent that is mistakenly seen in a rope can neither be bound by that rope nor driven away by it,

39. Or as darkness, terrified by the approaching dawn, might turn to the full moon, only to be swallowed by its rays,

40. So ignorance, abiding neither in the Self nor in sense perception, is twice invalidated. Perhaps, then, it can be understood only by logical inference.

41. What, then, is the true nature of ignorance? Can it be directly apprehended or must it be logically inferred from its effects?

42. Indeed, some claim that whatever can be apprehended by the various *pramanas*, like sense perception and its objects, is the effect of ignorance and not ignorance itself.

43. Just as, when a vine shoots upward from a seed, its sprout is not its seed but the effect of its seed;

44. Or as the auspicious or inauspicious forms seen in sleep are not sleep itself but the effects of sleep;

45. Or as two moons appearing in the sky are not defective eyesight but the effect of defective eyesight;

46. In the same way, the prover, the thing being proved, and the proof are the effect of ignorance and not ignorance itself.

47. So the various *pramanas* such as sense perception, being the effects of ignorance, cannot apprehend ignorance itself.

48. To which I reply: If the effects of ignorance are regarded as ignorance, then the senses by which they are apprehended are likewise the creations of ignorance.

49. But if what appears in a dream is illusory, do we say that the dreamer is illusory?

50. Can the effect of ignorance be ignorance? Can sugar savor its own sweetness? Can makeup put on makeup? Can a stake be impaled on itself?

51. If all effects were identical to their underlying cause, ignorance, then who could know anything whatsoever?

52. In such a condition, who could talk about a knower and a thing known? The *pramanas* themselves would be as substantial as fish in an imaginary lake.

53. And so, friends, what cannot be measured or defined by any proof is like a flower growing downward from the sky; it exists only in words.

54. Ignorance precludes the existence of any proof. How, then, can one sensibly expound its nature?

55. The existence of ignorance is impossible to prove either by sense perception or by inference, and is thereby refuted.

56. I am loath to believe in this ignorance, which neither causes anything nor is its own effect.

57. Ignorance can neither lull the Self asleep in his shining abode nor cause him to dream.

58. Nonetheless, some persist in saying that ignorance dwells in the pure state of the Self.

59. They claim that it does so in the same way that fire inheres in wood before two sticks are rubbed together.

60. To this I reply: when the pure Self even disdains the name "Self," how can ignorance expect to be greeted by it?

61. Can a flame be extinguished before it has been lit? Can one quit the shade of a tree whose seed has not yet sprouted?

62. Or spread oil on a body that has not yet been born? Or polish a mirror before its glass has been formed?

63. Or skim cream from milk that is still in a cow's udder?

64. If so, then ignorance can dwell in the Self—a Self that is so unspeakably pure that it remains prior to all names and forms. Not even its own name can touch it.

65. The incompatibility of ignorance with the Self should be obvious. Perhaps I am misguided to lend ignorance the semblance of existence by refuting it.

66.   If one were to persist in saying that ignorance dwells in
        the Self, which is beyond both being and nonbeing,

67.   It would be like saying that a nonexistent pitcher has been
        shattered into a thousand pieces or that death has been
        dealt a fatal blow;

68.   Or that consciousness has been knocked unconscious, or
        that darkness has plummeted into a dark well;

69.   Or that nonexistence has become embroiled in a street
        fight, that the hollow interior of a plantain tree has been
        emptied, that the sky can be cracked like a whip;

70.   Or that a corpse can be poisoned, a mute man silenced,
        unwritten letters erased.

71.   To claim that ignorance resides in the Self is to claim that
        they are identical.

72.   If so, then a barren woman can bear children, burned
        seeds sprout into trees, and darkness commingle with the
        light of the sun.

73.   No matter how hard you search for ignorance in the
        untainted intelligence of the Self, you shall never find it.

74.   If one were to stir milk in a pot in search of cream, would
        the cream rise to the top or be dissolved?

75.   If you wake yourself to catch hold of sleep, you will
        succeed only in dispelling it.

76.   Is it not insane to search for ignorance? To search or not
        to search for that which does not exist is equally absurd.

77. The city of the intelligence can never be illuminated by the false light of a concept like ignorance.

78. Have the eyes of insight ever been able to perceive ignorance either within the Self or, assuming it were possible, outside of it?

79. Ignorance can never anoint the countenance of judgment, discrimination, or right action. It cannot be established even in a dream. Thought, attempting to grasp it, loses itself instead.

80. In spite of this, do you still think you can discover a path to the ghost town of ignorance?

81. Go ahead! Build a city with rabbit horns and light it with rays from the new moon!

82. Celebrate! Weave bouquets of sky-flowers and bestow them on the offspring of barren women!

83. Our search for ignorance will be fulfilled when we fill the measuring glass of the sky with ghee extracted from a tortoise.

84. After having tried in vain, in so many ways, to discover ignorance, how long must we keep repeating that it does not exist?

85. As for me, not even in dreams would I think of repeating this empty word "ignorance." Nevertheless, I can imagine others having yet another thought about it.

86. Some might object: the ultimate transcendent Reality cannot become the seer and behold itself or any visible object.

87.   Therefore, it cannot cause the entire visible universe to
        arise before it, and acting as witness, survey all things.
        One must infer some other cause.

88.   The world that arises before our vision cannot also be
        visualized by the Self.

89.   Though ignorance is certainly invisible, it just as certainly
        exists, as is proven by inference from the visual world.

90.   If we see two moons in the sky, should we not infer
        defective eyesight as the cause of their appearance?

91.   If we were to see trees with abundant foliage growing out
        of a patch of dry ground, would we not infer that their
        hidden roots were drawing up water from below?

92.   Just so, ignorance can be readily inferred from the
        appearance of the visible world.

93.   Sleep not only vanishes as soon as one awakens, but it is
        also unknown to the one who sleeps; still, its existence is
        inferred from the memory of dreams.

94.   And so, in conclusion, if the visible universe appears,
        superimposed upon the formless Self, we must infer
        ignorance as its cause.

95.   To such a disputant, I would eagerly reply: How can
        knowledge of objects be called ignorance? Can that which
        gives light properly be called darkness?

96.   Can that be called collyrium which, applied to objects,
        makes them brighter and more lustrous than the moon?

97.　Asserting that ignorance is the cause of knowledge makes no more sense than claiming the full moon to be the cause of darkness.

98.　The belief that this world is the manifestation of ignorance is as logical as the claim that water burns in the form of fire.

99.　Can poison lovingly transform itself to ambrosia? If so, should we still call it poison?

100.　Why let loose an imaginary flood of ignorance when the light of knowledge reveals all that appears before us?

101.　If we call the apprehension of the visible universe "ignorance," what, then, since the Self is revealed neither by knowledge nor ignorance, is the function of knowledge?

102.　The Self does not become anything other than himself. He does not know himself as an object. All the means of knowledge disappear in him.

103.　He does not act in such a way as to cause us to say he exists. Likewise, there is no reason to call him nonexistent.

104.　In truth, the Self is, as he is independent of any external object. He sees without himself becoming the object of another's seeing. The fact that we cannot see him does not nullify his capacity as seer.

105.　He silently endures the conviction of the nihilists who believe he is nothing, nor is he vexed by those who would endow him with attributes.

106. Does the Omniscient One, who is the witness of even the void of deep sleep, fail to comprehend this? Though invisible himself, he is the ground of all that is visible.

107. The Vedas, which are unwilling to name him the Self, nonetheless refer to him as "not this, not this," as that which is beyond all that is knowable.

108. Is there any object that the sun cannot reveal? But can it reveal the Self? Can the Self be contained beneath the vault of the sky?

109. The ego considers the body, a sackful of bones, to be the true "I" and spurns the all-pervasive Self.

110. The intellect, which is able to grasp everything knowable, cannot grasp the Self. The mind is able to imagine everything it pleases—everything, that is, except the Self.

111. The senses, which scrape their famished mouths against the parched, rocky ground of sense objects, cannot taste the sweetness of the Self.

112. Is it possible to apprehend in its totality the Self that has filled its belly by consuming all that exists and all that does not exist?

113. Just as the tongue cannot taste itself, the Self cannot know itself as an object.

114. As soon as knowledge, with its brood of names and forms, draws near the Self, she realizes her ignorance with respect to it, loses heart, and turns back out of dread.

115. When one has no desire to see one's own face, why should others seek to gaze upon it?

116.   Is a person who inserts a stick into a cat's cradle surprised that, when the strings are loosened, the cradle comes apart and the stick falls from it?

117.   One who scrupulously measures the length of his shadow before attempting to leap over it cannot be supposed to have a true understanding of the nature of a shadow.

118.   Similarly, one who, after repeated attempts to comprehend the Self, imagines he has reached some definite conclusion, can only have failed to understand its nature.

119.   When words themselves recoil from the Self, how can the intellect, which functions by means of words, apprehend him as an object?

120.   With respect to the power of reason, when its blindness comes to an end, even its vision merges with the pure Self.

121.   Relative knowledge cannot touch the Self, which cannot experience itself as an object of perception.

122.   Where perception itself has disappeared, who can encounter whom, and from where can a glance of recognition flash forth?

123.   Rolling aside the obstacle of relative understanding, he [the Self] has opened the doors of his mansion through which his light pours.

124.   Though innumerable visions and forms may arise, the one Self is the substratum of all.

125.   The Self is so enamored with the manifold glory of his vision that an infinite variety of objects, each one different

from the last, are reflected like gems on the mirror of his awareness.

126.   He is so generous, so magnanimous, that he clothes his refined sight with garments that he changes at every instant.

127.   Regarding all created objects as dull and outworn, he constantly presents fresh and newly created objects before his effulgent vision.

128.   The Self assumes the role of subject by regaling himself at every moment with new objects of apprehension.

129.   Feeling constrained by his pristine dignity, the Self girds his loins and becomes the multifarious universe consisting of subjects and objects.

130.   This is the way of omniscience: though the pure Self is always full to the brim, he knows himself only as the master of his own house, only in the form of the universe that he has created.

131.   When that Pure Consciousness, in which knowledge and ignorance embrace each other and vanish, opens his eyes, he encounters himself in the form of visible objects.

132.   As soon as he beholds the visible world, he delights in it as its witness, and his delight pervades the entire vision that he unfolds before him.

133.   As the interplay of seer and seen continues, their underlying unity is never disrupted, just as the unity of a face is not disrupted by being seen in a mirror.

134.   A horse remains standing whether sleeping or waking.

135. Water sports with itself, assuming the form of waves. Just so, the Supreme Reality gleefully sports with itself.

136. Fire weaves garlands of its myriad flames, but does it thereby become different from itself?

137. Is the sun divorced from the rays that so abundantly pour from it?

138. Is the unity of the moon compromised because it is enveloped by light?

139. A lotus blossom contains a thousand petals, but it is still one blossom.

140. The mythological king Sahasrarjuna had one thousand hands; can we properly surmise that he was five hundred people?

141. Many strands may be woven on one loom, yet all are made of the same cotton.

142. No matter how many words a language contains, it is still only one language.

143. Innumerable leaves sprout from one tree; countless waves dance in one ocean; all objects and images arise from one Witness and are not different from him.

144. You may crumble a lump of sugar into a thousand bits, but you will still be left with nothing but sugar.

145. Similarly, though he perceives manifold images and manifests himself as countless objects, the Self does not thereby become different from himself.

146. Though he fills the entire universe, the unity of the Self is not lost.

147. A silk sari may be dyed many colors; still, it contains only thread.

148. In truth, the Self can see his creation even with his eyes closed.

149. It is as if a banyan tree, remaining just a seed, could simultaneously unfold into its full majestic form.

150. If he vehemently desires no longer to see, he withdraws into himself and reposes there.

151. His state then resembles vision when it has withdrawn into itself after the eyelids are closed;

152. Or the fullness of the ocean before the moon has arisen, or the repose of a tortoise who has retracted his limbs;

153. Or the stillness of the new moon before it has begun to wax once again.

154. The Self has been falsely called "the destroyer" when he withdraws both the seer and the seen; in truth, he is merely resting within himself.

155. All that exists is the Self. When he withdraws into himself, what remains to be seen, and by whom? The state in which he sees nothing is his unfathomable sleep.

156. When eventually he proclaims to himself, "Enough of this state of non-perception," he shines forth as his own object.

157.   The Self is the eternal perceiver and the eternally perceived. Do we need some further principle to account for him?

158.   Does the relationship between the sky and space, the air and touch, light and brightness, need to be newly established?

159.   The Self, shining as the universe, beholds the universe. When there is no universe, he perceives its nonexistence.

160.   And if the existence and nonexistence of the universe should merge, he would be the seer of this state as well.

161.   Are the coolness and whiteness of camphor intrinsic, or due to some other source, like the moonlight? Likewise, the intrinsic nature of the Self requires no external aid to become what he is, the Absolute Seer.

162.   What more can be said? Whatever his state, the Self is always beholding himself.

163.   He is like a man who perceives various lands by the powerful light of his imagination and travels through each one of them, relishing every sight.

164.   That same light dwells within all. No wonder that when one presses one's closed eyelid, a pure shining star of light vibrates within.

165.   When always and everywhere one Pure Consciousness beholds itself, why summon the specter of "superimposition?"

166.   Does one cover a jewel with shining foil? Does one paint gold with gold enamel?

167. Does sandalwood wear perfume? Does nectar serve itself nectar? Does sugar have a sweet tooth?

168. Is camphor whitened by chalk? Is fire heated by fire?

169. As a creeping vine, twisting about itself, is one with the bower it forms, or as a lamp is wholly suffused with its own light,

170. So Pure Consciousness is filled with its own spirit and vibrates in the form of the seer and the seen.

171. The Self naturally perceives himself without indebtedness to any other.

172. Moreover, seeing or not seeing are one to him. Does the moon care if it is darkened or bright?

173. If he desires that seeing should cease, the state of seeing nothing is instantly attained.

174. For an instant, the Self shines forth as an object of perception. But when the seer and the seen meet, both disappear.

175. The seer suffuses the object, whereupon both perception and the perceived vanish, and only their underlying essence remains.

176. Wherever and whenever the seer and seen meet, they melt in their mutual embrace, and both are dissolved.

177. When fire and camphor are brought together, fire does not turn into camphor, nor does camphor turn into fire. They completely interpenetrate, and each is wholly consumed.

178. When one is subtracted from one, the result is zero. Similarly, when the seer and the seen coalesce, each is subtracted from the other, and nothing remains.

179. If one were to attempt to wrestle with one's reflection in the water, both wrestler and reflection would be swallowed together.

180. When perception vanishes, the perceiver and the perceived unite and likewise vanish.

181. The eastern and western seas are separate as long as they do not mingle; as soon as they intermingle only water remains.

182. At every moment, some new expression of the same triad —the perceiver, perception, and the perceived—keeps arising. Do they constantly need to be analyzed?

183. Like the simultaneous opening and closing of the eyelids of the Ultimate Reality, the seer and the seen constantly swallow each other and emit each other as opposites.

184. How astonishing! When his eyes are closed, the Self becomes a seer; when they are open, the seer and all that is seen disappear.

185. The natural state of the Self lies in the interval between the destruction of the seer and the seen and their revival.

186. Such a state is like the surface of the water when one wave has just subsided and another is about to arise,

187. Or like that moment when sleep has just ended but we have not yet fully awakened.

188.   If you wish to conceive it, think of sight when it ceases to regard one object and, not yet resting on another, hovers in the gap between visions;

189.   Or think of sunset, of the horizon that flares as it fades from sight, just before night has risen;

190.   Or think of the moment when you have just inhaled a breath and are about to exhale;

191.   Or think of an individual when all of his senses are enjoying their objects simultaneously.

192.   The ultimate state of the Self is like this. It abides between seeing and not seeing.

193.   Does the Self see itself? Can a mirror admire its own spotless surface?

194.   With the help of a mirror, a face can regard itself, but can it still see itself when the mirror is removed?

195.   The sun makes everything visible, but can it witness the glory of its own rising and setting?

196.   Can juice drink itself, or refrain from drinking itself? It can do neither. It is just juice.

197.   In the same way, the Self, being vision itself, is neither seeing nor not seeing. He is the cause of both.

198.   Perception itself cannot perceive itself. Well, then, the Self must be non-perception.

199.   But how can non-perception perceive itself? Well, then, he must be perception.

200. And so perception and non-perception dwell happily together in the Self while constantly destroying and giving rise to each other.

201. If seeing were able to see itself, it would be the same as not seeing.

202. If the Self, who absents himself from seeing and not seeing, sees, then who has seen what?

203. If the visible world appears, then how can it be said that the seer has not perceived it?

204. Indeed, its appearance is seen, but in reality the seen is nothing but the seer. And again, that to which existence cannot be attributed cannot be seen.

205. A face is always a face. Its appearance in a mirror changes nothing.

206. Seeing oneself in a mirror is like being asleep and seeing oneself in a dream.

207. If one who is asleep dreams that he has traveled a great distance in a chariot, has he really been borne any distance at all?

208. If he dreams that two headless beggars are ruling the kingdom, does this mean that the king has in fact been overthrown?

209. The situation of a person in a dream does not change by virtue of his dreaming; when he wakens, he finds it the same.

210. The suffering of one perishing of thirst remains the same after he sees a mirage as before.

211. If a person strikes up a conversation with his own shadow, does he learn anything new?

212. Similarly, the seer, becoming the seen and revealing it to himself, actually reveals nothing new.

213. When the seen is nothing but the seer, can the seer be affected by the revelation of the seen? Does he become absent to himself when the seen disappears?

214. Does a face become superfluous when it sees itself in a mirror, or does the face remain as it is, rendering its reflected image superfluous?

215. The Self is not diminished if he is not revealed to himself; nonetheless, any constraint against his revealing himself would be equally pointless.

216. The Self abides happily in his own state without becoming a seer. Why, then, should he condescend to become the seen?

217. To try to manifest what is self-manifestly real would be not only redundant but futile.

218. Though a rope may appear to be a snake, it remains a rope. Similarly, it is the seer that really exists even in the appearance of the seen.

219. When a mirror is placed before a face, the image of that face unmistakably appears in it, yet the face itself does not change, and remains where it is.

220. Between the seer and the seen, the seer is primary. The seen is his manifestation.

221. Though redundant, appearances do manifest, and thus would seem to have some existence.

222. If someone remains other than what he sees, we can say that he sees it.

223. But the Self, whether he sees or does not see, whether he remains one or becomes many, sees nothing other than himself.

224. Whether it is or is not reflected in a mirror, a face remains as it is in itself.

225. Whether revealed by wakefulness or concealed by sleep, a person remains the same.

226. Whether or not he becomes manifest, the seer remains unchanged.

227. A king does not need to be reminded, "You are a king!" in order to retain his sovereignty.

228. Nor is there any diminution of his dignity if he is not so reminded.

229. Similarly, whether manifest or unmanifest, the status of the Self is unaltered, and he remains naturally in his own state.

230. What other extraneous thing is madly trying to reveal the Self to itself? Of what use is a mirror when there is no one to gaze in it?

231. Does a lamp cause the person who lights it, or does the person cause the light? The existence of any cause is due to the Self.

232. Are the flames whose light reveals a fire any different from that fire?

233. Whatever we call a cause is manifested and revealed by him alone. By his very nature, the Self is both the seer and the object seen.

234. The Self is self-illumining; he and no other is the cause for his seeing himself.

235. Whatever form appears manifests only through him.

236. Gold shines, whether in the form of a bracelet or of a solid lump, because both are nothing but gold, and it is the nature of gold to shine.

237. In the rushing current of a river or in the surging waves of the sea, there is nothing but water. Similarly, whatever is brought into existence is nothing but the Self.

238. The existence of camphor may be inferred through smell, touch, or sight, but in and of itself camphor is just camphor.

239. Likewise, the Self experiences himself just as he is.

240. Whether he exists as the seer or appears as the seen, nothing becomes manifest without him.

241. Whether the Ganges flows as a river or merges with the ocean, its water remains nothing but water.

242. Whether in liquid or frozen form, ghee remains ghee. To inquire regarding a distinction is meaningless.

243. A fire and its flames are not two different things. Together, they constitute fire.

244.   To discriminate between the state of the seer and that of the seen is futile; it is the one state of the Self that pulsates everywhere.

245.   For the supreme vibration of the Self, nothing exists that is not that vibration. So though the Self is said to see, is there really anything separate from himself to see?

246.   In ordinary seeing, the seer and the seen are separate in space. But space itself is subsumed in the vibration of the seer, who sees nothing but that vibration.

247.   His vision is like ripples overlapping ripples, like gold plated with gold, like eyesight bewitched with the power of sight.

248.   It is like melody superadded to itself, like perfume sprinkled on perfume, like perfect contentment serving itself the dish of contentment.

249.   It is like sugar sweetened with sugar, like the golden Mount Meru being gilded, like a fire encircled by its own flames.

250.   What more can I say? When the sky reposes on the divan of the sky, who should sleep and who should wake?

251.   When he sees himself, it is as though he sees nothing— and this not seeing is his natural way of seeing.

252.   Here talk is not tolerated; knowledge gains no entrance; experience cannot boast of its greatness.

253.   His seeing himself is like no one seeing nothing.

254.   In short, the Self is illumined by the Self. He wakens himself without awakening.

255. When he desires to see himself, he manifests the various states of the seer and the seen without disturbing his own condition.

256. When he desires to see nothing, his not seeing itself becomes a kind of seeing; and in this seeing both seeing and not seeing vanish.

257. Though he may expand into innumerable forms or contract into his formless state, his perfect unity is not affected in the slightest.

258. The sun can never apprehend darkness. What need has he to hear prattle about light?

259. Just as the sun is affected by neither darkness nor light, in the presence of either, the Self remains as he is in his glorious effulgence.

260. Whatever position the Self may assume, he never strays from himself.

261. Though countless waves arise and subside in the ocean, it does not become other than what it is.

262. The glory of the Self surpasses even that of the sun, because the sun's rays depart from it.

263. If cotton buds are not broken, no cloth can be produced, but the Self produces the whole world while remaining entirely intact.

264. The Self is not like a lump of unworked gold which, if it remains as it is, cannot assume the form of ornaments that adorn the body.

265.   No individual can be compared to the Self, for no individual can travel from country to country without traversing the intervening space.

266.   And so his play is without parallel. He can be compared only to himself.

267.   Though the idol of the Goddess Ambika[17] is made of effulgent gold, she is nonetheless called "the dark one."

268.   The Self incessantly devours mouthfuls of his own light. Though his meal is inexhaustible, the size of his belly never changes.

269.   The Self, through his incomparable sport or play, is the sovereign of his own kingdom.

270.   To call his sport "ignorance" is to abandon all pretense of logic. Can we safely tolerate such idle chatter?

271.   Is that which illumines properly called ignorance? Then a miner's lamp, seeking out buried wealth, is a lump of coal.

272.   In reality everything from Lord Shiva to the lowliest clod of clay is illumined by the Self.

273.   Because of him alone, knowledge knows, sight sees, and light enlightens.

274.   O, what mean-spirited scoundrel has besmirched him with the word "ignorance"! Let him try to tie up the sun in a filthy old sack!

275.   To scratch the letter "A" before *jnana*[18] so as to enhance its greatness—what a curious way to augment a word's meaning. Such addition is more like subtraction.

276. Why place fire inside a cardboard box when that box will instantly go up in flames?

277. Why so much sententious chatter about the doctrine of ignorance when the whole universe is the vibration of knowledge?

278. Such talk is twice sinful; it is both blasphemous and false. How can knowledge be called ignorance?

279. And it merely compounds the blasphemy to say that ignorance is the vibration of knowledge. If so, how can knowledge be called knowledge?

280. Let it be seen, through the very illumination of the Self, that the Self illumines himself in countless forms.

281. How can ignorance, which pales before the beacon of inquiry, acquire vision and behold itself in the visible world?

282. If ignorance were to proclaim that it gives birth to the world through ignorance, and were to try to argue that the appearance of that world is established by ignorance, I would reply:

283. Knowledge of the world, on the contrary, emphatically proves the nonexistence of ignorance, because knowledge is not a quality or an attribute of the supposed substance ignorance and cannot be associated with it.

284. Knowledge can no more be a quality of ignorance than pearls can be formed from water or a light lit with ashes.

285. The sky could sooner be turned into a stone, or the moon exhale fire, than ignorance could radiate the light of knowledge.

286.　It would certainly be surprising if a fatal poison could be skimmed from an ocean of milk, but would it not be still more surprising if pure nectar could be distilled from a deadly poison?

287.　Just as knowledge cannot be produced as a quality of ignorance, so ignorance cannot be produced as a quality of knowledge. Even if it were to so arise, it would vanish at the instant of its birth, and knowledge alone would remain.

288.　The sun shines as the sun; the moon shines as the moon; a lamp shines as a lamp.

289.　So the light of knowledge shines as knowledge. And the light of the supreme substance—the Self—shines as the world, which is nothing but that light.

290.　The Upanishads declare contentedly that what exists is illuminated by the light of the Self. Are the scriptures without purpose?

291.　The light of the Self alone, in order to relish its beauty, causes that beauty to appear.

292.　The Self is self-illumined; to regard ignorance as the cause of its illumination is utterly unreasonable.

293.　In sum, no matter how hard we search for ignorance, our search will prove futile. We can never find it.

294.　Though it were to travel to the very abode of light, the sun would find no darkness.

295.　Try to catch sleep in a bag, and you will fail to catch even wakefulness; but you will never fail to remain, nonetheless, who you are.

VIII. THE UNREALITY OF KNOWLEDGE

1. As for ourselves, we possess neither knowledge nor ignorance. Our guru has established us in our true nature.

2. If we attempt to see our own state, seeing itself is abashed, and retreats. How, then, are we to know ourselves?

3. Fortunately, our guru has made us so free that no distinction can contain us. We cannot even contain ourselves!

4. We are not restricted to being the Self, nor is our state disturbed by self-knowledge. Not even liberation can alter it.

5. No word that describes us has ever been heard. No eye that perceives us has ever been seen.

6. Who could possibly perceive us, or enjoy us as an object, when we cannot even perceive ourselves?

7. It is no wonder that we remain neither concealed nor manifest; the wonder is that we somehow still manage to exist.

8. How, then, can we describe in words the state that has been bestowed on us by Sri Nivritti?

9. Does ignorance dare approach us? Can *Maya* outlast her own death?

10. Where ignorance gains no entry, knowledge becomes irrelevant.

11. When it is night, one needs a lamp. But it is useless to light one when there is sun.

12.   When the chimera of ignorance has been dispelled, knowledge also disappears.

13.   Knowledge and ignorance arise as mutually dependent opposite terms. When one is destroyed, both are destroyed.

14.   If a husband and wife decided to cut off their heads and place them on each other's necks, instead of effecting a transposition, they would end their own lives.

15.   If a person could see in the dark, a lamp would be of no use to him, and darkness would not impede him. Both would be recognized as equally ineffectual.

16.   The utter non-cognition that is called ignorance obviously lacks any power of comprehension.

17.   Alas, the knowledge that supposedly illumines and comprehends ignorance has nothing to illumine, and itself becomes nescient, thereby canceling itself.

18.   He who knows does not know, and he who does not know, knows. Where, then, do knowledge and ignorance dwell?

19.   Through the grace of the guru, the light of spiritual insight dawns in the sky of Pure Consciousness, consuming both the day of knowledge and the night of ignorance.

IX.   THE NATURAL STATE OF DEVOTION

1.   Now fragrance becomes the nose that inhales it, ears become the music that they hear, and eyes become the mirrors that they behold.

2.   Fans become soft breezes, and heads assume the form of *champa*[19] flowers.

3.   Tongues become flavor, the lotus opens into the form of the sun, and *chakor* birds become the moon by whose light they fly.

4.   Bees turn into flowers, young women become their lovers, sleepers become the beds upon which they recline.

5.   The blossoms of the mango become the cuckoo and delight in themselves, and the body becomes the wind that cools it.

6.   Gold, fashioning ornaments of itself, is dazzled by its own charming appearance.

7.   In the same way, the enjoyer, the means of enjoyment, and the enjoyed, the perceiver, perception, and the perceived are merged in the seamless unity of the Self.

8.   Just as a *shevanti*[20] flower blossoms into a thousand petals without ceasing to be a shevanti flower,

9.   So the citadel of stillness remains silent though the auspicious drums of countless new experiences may beat.

10.   The senses of the seer may rush simultaneously to greet their respective objects,

11. But no sooner is contact made than they vanish within him.

12. Whether gold is worked into the form of a brooch, a bracelet, or an earring, their purchaser buys nothing but gold.

13. A hand that reaches to gather the ripples in a stream gathers nothing but water.

14. Whether experienced as touch by the hand, as an image to the eye, or as sweetness by the tongue, camphor is always experienced as fragrance.

15. Just so, the Self alone vibrates in the form of the sensible manifold.

16. Whether one attempts to grasp sense objects directly through organs of action like the hands, or more subtly through the senses, or indirectly through words,

17. Since all are the Self, and the Self cannot grasp itself as an object, the instant that contact occurs, the sense object vanishes.

18. As all of the parts of the sugar cane are contained in its juice, and as all of its phases are subsumed by the light of the full moon,

19. Or as rainwater dissolves in the ocean, just so, upon meeting, both the senses and their objects dissolve in the Self.

20. The silence of the meditation of one who has realized this state of unity remains undisturbed even while he says whatever he wishes.

21.   Even though he performs countless actions, his actionless
        state remains unimpaired.

22.   His vision is one with its object. When his sense of sight
        apprehends its object, it gains nothing at all.

23.   When the sun attempts to embrace the darkness, it
        succeeds only in dispelling it and remains just as it is.

24.   When a person springs from a bed to meet the figments
        of a dream, he finds himself alone.

25.   In the same way, when one who has attained the vision of
        unity seems to be enjoying sense objects, one cannot
        really know whether he is enjoying them or not.

26.   Would it make sense for the moon to gather its own light?
        The knower of the Self has nothing to gain from
        remembering sense objects.

27.   Likewise, to one who has attained the state of a *Siddha*,[21]
        the yoga of the restraint of the senses is as lusterless as the
        moon in broad daylight.

28.   For him, there is neither action nor inaction. All is the
        spontaneous experience of the Self.

29.   The fully integrated one enters the courtyard of duality of
        his own accord. His experience of unity is only intensified
        through the experience of diversity.

30.   To one who has attained true wisdom, the enjoyment of
        sense objects is even sweeter than the bliss of liberation. In
        the house of the devotee, the lover and his God
        experience their sweet union.

31.   In truth, whether he walks the streets or remains still, he always remains in his own abode.

32.   Though he may perform any action, he has no goal to attain. Even without doing anything, he achieves his object.

33.   There is no room in his awareness for either memory or forgetfulness. In such a condition, his behavior is indeed uncommon!

34.   His own sweet will is his rule of conduct. His meditation is whatever he happens to be doing. The glory of liberation is merely the mat upon which he sits.

35.   God himself has become the devotee. The destination has become the path. The whole universe is one with his solitude.

36.   According to his will, he assumes the role of God or of devotee. Even in inactivity, he enjoys the sovereignty of a king.

37.   The temple of his body has merged with the all-pervasive God. For him, time and space have vanished.

38.   God contains God within himself. There is no room in him for either the Goddess or for retainers.

39.   Should a desire for the relation of guru and disciple arise in him, God himself must assume both roles.

40.   Yogic practices, such as mantra repetition, meditation, and unwavering faith, are not different from God.

41.   In him, God worships God by means of God: this is his only offering.

42. A temple, its idol, and the attendants of the deity are all carved from the same rock. Why should there be outward performance of the acts of devotion when God alone is everywhere?

43. Spreading in the forms of foliage, flowers, and fruits, a tree remains simply a tree.

44. Whether or not one who is dumb chooses to observe a vow of silence is irrelevant. Whether or not a *Siddha* chooses to worship, he rests in his divinity.

45. Is there any point in offering rice to an idol of the Goddess formed out of rice?

46. Will the flame of a lamp grow dark if we do not beseech it to wear a garment of light?

47. Will the moon grow dark if we do not implore her to dress in moonlight?

48. Fire, by its very nature, is hot. Is there any reason to think of heating or of not heating it?

49. The *Siddha*, by his very nature, is Lord Shiva himself. He is the essence of devotion when he is worshipping and when he is not worshipping.

50. Now the lights of action and inaction have been extinguished, and worship and non-worship, occupying the same seat, have the same dish before them.

51. Regarding one in such a state, the injunctions of the sacred texts of the Upanishads are a censure—although, when applied to him, even censure itself becomes a hymn of praise!

52. With respect to him, both praise and blame are reduced to silence. Indeed, any talk of him is nothing but silence.

53. Wherever he walks, he is on a pilgrimage to Shiva; and yet on that pilgrimage, he is going nowhere at all.

54. Isn't it a wonder—to one in his state, walking and sitting still have become the same thing!

55. If his sight happens to fall on any object whatsoever, he experiences the joy of beholding Shiva.

56. Still, should Lord Shiva himself appear before him, it would be as if he had seen nothing. Whatever he sees is already contained within him.

57. If a ball could toss itself, strike against itself, and rebound, enraptured by its own bliss,

58. Its spontaneous play would be an image of the utterly free existence of a *Siddha*.

59. Such complete spontaneity is the way of natural devotion. Neither can the hand of action touch it nor knowledge penetrate it.

60. Neither arising nor subsiding, forever resounding in itself, such devotion has no end. What bliss can be compared to it?

61. This is the wonderful secret of natural devotion; it is the point where yoga and knowledge unite.

62. Shiva and Vishnu[22] merge in one body; even their nominal difference dissolves.

63.   Shiva and Shakti, who are accustomed to swallowing and emitting each other, are both subsumed in the state of natural devotion.

64.   In such a state, *para*, having consumed all other levels of speech and their objects, as well as their speakers, itself rests in blissful sleep.

65.   O blessed and mighty Lord! You have made us the sole sovereign of the kingdom of supreme bliss!

66.   How wonderful it is that you have wakened the wakeful, lulled the sleeping to sleep, and brought us to the realization of who we already are!

67.   We all belong to you, and out of your magnanimity and love for us, you call us your own.

68.   You do not take anything from anyone, and you give without giving yourself away. O Supreme Guru, who can comprehend the manner in which you enjoy your greatness?

69.   As the guru, you are immensely weighty, yet you become as light as a buoy to save your drowning disciples. This paradox is grasped only by those who have received your grace.

70.   If your unity could be disturbed by your sharing it with your disciples, would all of the scriptures extol you?

71.   O noble one, it is your pleasure to become our nearest and dearest by destroying our sense of difference from you. In this, how supremely fortunate we are!

X.   BLESSING TO THE WORLD

1.   O, Shri Nivrittinath! You have blessed me with such supreme bliss. Should I relish it within myself alone?

2.   The Supreme Lord has endowed the sun with a fountain of light that illumines the whole world.

3.   Was nectar granted to the moon for it to hoard? Does the ocean grant its moisture to the clouds for them to keep?

4.   The light of a lamp is meant to illumine the whole household. The dazzling light of the sky shines upon all.

5.   The power of the moon causes tides to swell in the unfathomable ocean. The sweet influence of spring inspires trees to offer their flowers and fruits.

6.   In the same way, it is an open secret that your inspiration is the source of all that I have spoken. None of these words are my own.

7.   But why should I try to explain myself? My words only occlude the full radiance of my master's glory.

8.   All that has been said is self-evident. Are words required to illumine the self-illumined?

9.   Were I to have kept silent, would people thereby have been prevented from meeting one another?

10.   When one person meets and beholds the other, it is self-evident that each is both the seer and the seen.

11.   The nature of Absolute Consciousness is no more mysterious than this. It is clear before one even speaks of it.

12. If a person were to ask, "Why, then, have you undertaken this work?" I would reply, "I am describing what is self-evident only out of my love for it."

13. We enjoy the flavor of our favorite dish anew each time we taste it. For this reason I have described what is self-evident.

14. It is not I who divulged the secret of the Absolute. It soundlessly proclaims itself.

15. Wherever we turn, we can see nothing but our own Self. Pervading all, there is nothing that can either conceal or reveal us.

16. What sermon should one preach to oneself? Does one lose anything by remaining silent?

17. Therefore my speech has become the deepest silence. It vanishes like a picture of a fish drawn with a finger upon the surface of the water.

18. Not even the ten Upanishads can draw near to the Absolute. Understanding itself dissolves in the attempt to fathom it.

19. Jnaneshwar says: This is the nectar of spiritual experience. Let even the liberated drink a full draught.

20. The state of emancipation has its charms, but the nectar of spiritual experience is so pure and sweet that even the state of liberation itself eagerly desires a taste of it.

21. Should I, who have a vision of the sun, praise the brightness of the full moon night?

22. The beauty of youth abides in a young girl, but it blossoms forth when she is united with her beloved.

23.   With the advent of spring, the trees begin to kiss the sky, their branches laden with flowers and fruits.

24.   Likewise, I have served the dish of my spiritual experience in the form of this talk.

25.   The difference between those who are liberated, eager for liberation, or still in bondage remains only so long as they have not tasted the nectar of spiritual experience.

26.   As streams that flow into the Ganges become the Ganges, or as darkness, encountering the sun, becomes light;

27.   Or as talk of the different qualities of metal ceases when it has been transformed into pure gold by the philosopher's stone;

28.   So those who enter into the inner sanctum of these words are like rivers whose waters mingle with the ocean.

29.   As all of the letters in the alphabet coincide in the syllable "*Om*," so the entire animate and inanimate universe abides in the Self.

30.   There is nothing that is not Shiva. Everything is pervaded by the Lord, the supreme Self of all.

31.   Jnaneshwar says: Let the whole world enjoy the feast of the nectar of spiritual experience.

AMRITANUBHAV

ABOUT GEORGE FRANKLIN

 In his youth, George Franklin studied literature at Harvard, Brown, and Columbia. At the age of 18, he began writing poetry. From then until the end of his life, he continued to dedicate himself to crafting his own poetry as well as studying and writing about poetry and the great poets he most highly esteemed.

A second great interest took root in Mr. Franklin at age 23, when he met a great Indian guru, from whom he received a powerful spiritual awakening. His guru had an ashram in Maharashtra, India, where he taught the practice and philosophy of Indian mystical and devotional traditions, including Kashmir Shaivism.

Under his guru's guidance, and following his own inclinations as well, Mr. Franklin became a student of Eastern and Western mystical traditions. He ultimately felt his own two greatest interests in life—poetry and mysticism—came together in the work of the great Maharashtrian poet-saint Jnaneshwar Maharaj. Before rendering the saint's work *Amritanubhav* into poetic English, Franklin went on pilgrimage to Jnaneshwar's *samadhi* shrine in Alandi to offer his devotion and experience the blessing of Jnaneshwar's sacred spirit.

During his final years, suffering from multiple debilitating illnesses that consigned him to a nursing home, Mr. Franklin arose daily before dawn to produce a series of astonishingly virtuosic books of poetry, memoir, and literary criticism. He died at age 71, leaving behind a triumphant legacy in the form of his writing.

AMRITANUBHAV

ENDNOTES - GLOSSARY

1 *Samadhi* in this context is the final merging with the divine, leaving the physical body behind; sometimes called *mahasamadhi*, or the great merging.

2 A German scholar of medieval Marathi, Ahim Rheinhhart (sic). If any reader knows the whereabouts of this scholar, we would love to contact him. For now, we offer him our heartfelt thanks.

3 Shiva and Shakti represent the two distinct but inseparable aspects of the sacred, personified in male and female forms.

4 *Shambu* is another name for Shiva.

5 Two of the four levels of speech, *para* and *vaikhari*. See note 12 below.

6 While the sacred mantra is often represented as *Om,* in Sanskrit it is comprised of the three letters *A, U,* and *M.*

7 The word *sadhana* refers to the spiritual practices that one performs on the path to enlightenment. They may differ from tradition to tradition.

8 *Maya* is considered the force that conceals reality; often personified.

9 *Brahman* is the name for the Absolute; there is nothing higher than Brahman.

10 In the Indian philosophical systems, *pramanas* are the means or sources of knowledge used to determine what is true, such as direct sense perception, inference, and the testimony of past or present reliable sources such as scriptures. (Source: Chat-GPT)

11 This is a play on the word *nivritti*, which in addition to being Jnaneshwar's guru's name also means renunciation, turning inwards away from the world.

12 In Indian philosophy, the four levels of speech are:
Parā (or paravak) The transcendental level, representing the pure, undifferentiated consciousness.
Paśyantī: The visionary level, where ideas and intentions begin to form but are not yet articulated.
Madhyamā: The mental level, or thoughts prior to speech.
Vaikharī: The external level, where speech is articulated and expressed verbally. (Source: Chap-GPT)

13 *sattva* is one of the three *gunas*, or qualities of phenomena in Hindu philosophy, along with *rajas* and *tamas*. Sattva represents harmony, peacefulness, and virtue, etc. (*rajas* is passion or movement; *tamas* is ignorance or inertia.

14 The four bodies are defined in the yogic tradition as: the gross physical body; the subtle body of life energy and mental formations; the causal body, which is the seed of the subtle and gross bodies, made of pure ignorance; and the supra-causal body, transcendental, pure consciousness.

15 *sat-chit-anand* is the Sanskrit term meaning existence, consciousness, and bliss.

16 The *chakor* bird is a mythological bird in Hinduism, a partridge that feeds on moonbeams.

17 The Goddess Ambika is another name for the supreme goddess, *Mahadevi*.

18 In Sanskrit, one adds the letter "a" in front of a word as negation; *jnana* means knowledge, and therefore *ajnana* means ignorance.

19 The *champa* flower is a fragrant flower also known as a plumeria or frangipani flower.

20 The *shevanti* flower is a chrysanthemum.

21 A *Siddha* is one who has attained perfect enlightenment.

22 Vishnu is a god in the Hindu tradition, considered the preserver of the universe.